# Vladimir Mayakovsky

## Twayne's World Authors Series
### Russian Literature

Charles A. Moser, Editor
*George Washington University*

TWAS 706

VLADIMIR MAYAKOVSKY
(1918)
Photograph reproduced from Mayakovsky's
*Collected Works: Polnoe sobranie sochineniy.*
Vol. 2. Moscow, 1956.

# Vladimir Mayakovsky

## By Victor Terras
*Brown University*

*Twayne Publishers • Boston*

*Vladimir Mayakovsky*

Victor Terras

Copyright © 1983 by G. K. Hall & Company
All Rights Reserved
Published by Twayne Publishers
A Division of G. K. Hall & Company
70 Lincoln Street
Boston, Massachusetts 02111

Book Production by Marne B. Sultz

Book Design by Barbara Anderson

Printed on permanent/durable acid-free
paper and bound in the United States of
America.

**Library of Congress Cataloging in Publication Data**

Terras, Victor.
  Vladimir Mayakovsky.

  (Twayne's world authors series ; TWAS 706)
  Bibliography: p. 156
  Includes index.
  1. Mayakovsky, Vladimir, 1894–1930.
2. Poets, Russian—20th century—Biography.
I. Title.  II. Series.
PG3476.M312T4 1983      891.71′42      83–6185
ISBN 0–8057–6553–0

# Contents

*About the Author*
*Preface*
*Chronology*

## About the Author

Victor Terras was born and educated in Estonia. He came to this country in 1952 and received his Ph.D. in Russian literature from the University of Chicago in 1963. He has taught Russian language and literature at the University of Illinois (Urbana), the University of Wisconsin (Madison), and Brown University. He has published scholarly articles and reviews on several Russian poets and writers.

# *Preface*

Vladimir Mayakovsky (1893–1930), more than perhaps any other twentieth-century poet, has meant different things to different audiences. To the Western historian of literature, he is one of the most remarkable poets of the European avant-garde. To the literary historian in the Soviet Union, he is the greatest Soviet poet. To the student of Russian versification, he is by far the greatest challenge in the field. To many Russian poets he has been a model. Mayakovsky made his mark not only as a poet and playwright, but also as a cartoonist and all-purpose propagandist. He wrote a number of film scenarios and played the lead in several films. His voice was often heard on Soviet radio. He was a tireless traveler who gave countless poetry recitals and talks in the Soviet Union as well as abroad, including the United States. But most of all, Mayakovsky was a "star." Some of his contemporaries were almost certainly greater poets, but none of them remotely approached Mayakovsky's broad public appeal. He was a legend from the outset of his career, and everything he did later enhanced his image, which was much more than life size while he was living and grew to heroic proportions after his sensational suicide.

Mayakovsky's was a life packed with events and achievements. His *Collected Works* fill thirteen volumes. The literature about his life and works is so large that a complete bibliography would fill a solid volume. The present study can only outline the most important facets of Mayakovsky's life and manifold activities. It concentrates on Mayakovsky the poet, giving only cursory attention to his other achievements.

Mayakovsky remains a controversial figure. A free spirit and irrepressible bohemian before the Revolution, he "stepped on the throat of his own songs" and transformed himself into a willing tool of the Soviet regime—a literary hack, that is, said many contemporaries. Western critics have tended to downgrade his postrevolutionary work, while Soviet critics do the exact opposite. The fact is that the Soviet propaganda poet was at least as virtuosic as the free spirit of the prerevolutionary years, and probably more so. Questions regarding the dependence of an artist's greatness on the moral quality of his work and the connection between creative freedom and artistic excellence loom large in Mayakovsky's case.

In this short monograph I have tried to maintain a balance between Mayakovsky's life and work, between description and analysis, between presentation of bare fact and suggestion of problems. I have also tried to provide enough background information so that the reader may see Mayakovsky and his work in their historical context. I hope to have left the impression throughout that my treatment is rudimentary and that anyone who really wants to get to know Mayakovsky will have to pursue the various angles which I have tried to point out in this book.

Victor Terras

*Brown University*

# Chronology

"Decree No. 1 on the Democratization of Art." *Man* and *War and the World*. Writes several film scenarios and plays the lead in two films. 7 November, *Mystery-Bouffe* performed at the Petrograd Musical Theater to celebrate the first anniversary of the October Revolution.

1918–1919   Publishes poems in *Art of the Commune,* organ of the Department of Fine Arts (IZO) of the Peoples Commissariat of Public Education.

1919–1922   Works for the display windows of ROSTA, the Soviet wire service, as a cartoonist and writer of propaganda jingles.

1921   Spring, *150,000,000*.

1922   May, first trip abroad, to Riga, Latvia. October–December, visits Germany and France.

1923   March, First issue of *Lef* (1923–25). *About That* is printed in *Lef* and as a separate booklet.

1924   After Lenin's death, Mayakovsky reads portions of *Vladimir Ilich Lenin* to Russian audiences. October–December, in Paris.

1925   *Vladimir Ilich Lenin* printed in *Lef* and as a separate booklet. 4 June, opening of the Soviet pavilion of the Exhibition of Industrial Arts in Paris, at which Mayakovsky is present. 20 June–28 October, travels to and in North America. 19 December, reads his poem "Homeward Bound" to a Moscow audience.

1926   "To Sergei Esenin" and "How to Make Verse"; "Conversation with a Tax Collector about Poetry."

1927   January, first issue of *New Lef*. Travels to Poland, Germany, Czechoslovakia, and France. *Good! A Poem of October.*

1928   May–September, film *Dekabryukhov and Oktyabryukhov,* with scenario by Mayakovsky, flops in Kiev and Moscow. August, Mayakovsky relinquishes editorship of *New Lef*. Fall, brings back a Renault car from Paris. "A Letter to Comrade Kostrov from Paris, on the Nature of Love."

1929   13 February, *The Bedbug* performed in Moscow. 14 February, leaves for Paris and a vacation on the Côte d'Azur. September, refused a passport.

1930   30 January, *The Bathhouse* flops in Leningrad. 31 January, opening of Mayakovsky's exhibition "Twenty Years of Work" at the Writers Club in Moscow. February, applies for membership in Russian Association of Proletarian Writers. 5 March, exhibition transferred to Leningrad. 16 March, *The Bathhouse* opens in Moscow at Meyerhold's Theater. 14 April, Mayakovsky commits suicide.

# Chapter One
# A Biographical Survey

## The Early Years

Vladimir Vladimirovich Mayakovsky was born on 19 July 1893 in Bagdadi (now named Mayakovsky in his honor), a small village in western Georgia, where his father, Vladimir Konstantinovich, was a forester in the government service. Family life (there were two older sisters, Olga and Lyudmila) was warm and harmonious. Mayakovsky remained close to his mother, Aleksandra Alekseevna, into his adulthood. His father died in 1906 of blood poisoning from a cut on his finger. Subsequently, Mayakovsky had a lifelong fear of infection, and was a compulsive hand washer. When he called himself "a singer of boiled, and an implacable enemy of unboiled water"[1] in the poem which would be his own eulogy, he may have been thinking of something more than the posters he used to draw during the civil war years, urging people to boil their water before drinking it.

Volodya (hypocoristic for Vladimir) was a precocious child, both physically and mentally, and seemed much older than his age. He had started secondary school in nearby Kutais in the fall of 1902, but took little interest in his school work and his grades were consistently poor. Those were exciting times. The Russo-Japanese War began in January 1904, to be followed by the Revolution of 1905. Lyudmila, by then a student in Moscow, brought back political books and pamphlets, both legal and illegal. Volodya, now a third grader, loved the excitement of mass meetings, demonstrations, and revolutionary songs.

After her husband's death, Mrs. Mayakovsky decided to move to Moscow, where her elder daughter was studying and where she had managed to place her younger daughter in a private school for girls. Volodya entered the fourth grade of Moscow public secondary school number 5. Mayakovsky's childhood in Georgia seems to have left few traces. He spoke Georgian fluently and liked to speak the language whenever he met Georgians, but he never seems to have taken an interest in Georgian poetry. He was not the sort of person who should have grown up in a forester's family in rural Georgia. The beauty of the Caucasian landscape seems to have left no impression in young Mayakovsky's mind. As a poet and artist he either ignored or manipulated nature, though he always had a warm feeling for animals.

Mrs. Mayakovsky's modest pension was hardly adequate to support a family in Moscow, and her children soon began to contribute to the family budget. Olga and Volodya developed a skill at firing and coloring wooden objects—boxes, caskets, Easter eggs—which Lyudmila sold to stores. It is significant that Mayakovsky's first artistic endeavor was of a "commercial" variety. His mother reported another significant trait: young Volodya immediately became attracted to the movies. His road to poetry was unconventional and modern.

Mayakovsky appeared on the stage of history as early in his life as Russia's great poet Aleksandr Pushkin (1799–1837), who published his first poem at fourteen. Mayakovsky, however, made his first mark as a revolutionary rather than as a poet. Secondary school pupils often took an active interest in politics, illegal politics in particular. They formed groups which were in touch with the revolutionary underground and, being less conspicuous than adults, they were welcome as messengers, distributors of leaflets, and lookouts. Volodya seems to have taken up such activities soon after his enrollment in secondary school. By the fall of 1907, or early in 1908, according to other reports, young Mayakovsky, barely fourteen years old, was a full-fledged member of the Bolshevik faction of the Russian Social Democratic party and was soon elected to its Moscow committee. It must be noted, though, that local party membership in 1908 numbered in the dozens, and not in the hundreds or thousands. Also, the police had things well under control, as young Mayakovsky was soon to find out: the police records, including reports by undercover agents who had him under surveillance, are extant.

On 29 March 1908 Mayakovsky was arrested for the first time. The police had seized an illegal printing press of the Social Democratic party and Mayakovsky walked into the ensuing stakeout, carrying a stack of proclamations. A letter from his principal in response to an inquiry from the examining magistrate reveals that Vladimir Mayakovsky, a fifth grade pupil, "had been stricken from the school register as of 1 March 1908 for nonpayment of school fees." The examining magistrate eventually decided "to put said Mayakovsky under special police surveillance at his place of residence." On 30 August 1908 Mayakovsky was admitted to the preparatory class of the Stroganov School of Industrial Arts.

His second arrest, on 21 January 1909, may have been an accident. He had been seen with several members of the Socialist Revolutionary party who were suspected of involvement in "expropriations," that is, bank robberies as a means to replenish the party treasury, then fairly common occurrences. This time Mayakovsky was quite innocent and he was released, along with several other detainees, on 27 February.

His third arrest was more serious. He was involved with one I. I. Morchadze, a Georgian revolutionary who had participated in the "expropriation" of a Moscow bank, and also helped organize a successful jailbreak of political prisoners from the Moscow Prison for Women on 1 July 1909. On the next day Mayakovsky once more walked into a stakeout at the apartment of Morchadze's wife. He denied having any connection with the jailbreak.

Young Mayakovsky, a seasoned jailhouse lawyer at fifteen and fully cognizant of his rights, gave his jailers more trouble than they could handle. His warden's report, dated 17 August 1909, reads: "Vladimir Vladimirovich Mayakovsky, held in the prison under my administration, by his behavior incites other prisoners to disobedience toward prison officers, persistently demands free access to all cells, purporting to be the prisoners' 'spokesman'; whenever let out of his cell to go to the toilet or washroom, he stays out of his cell for half an hour, parading up and down the corridor."[2] The report ends with a "humble request to have Mayakovsky transferred to another prison." The request was granted. Other wardens must have been equally unhappy with Mayakovsky, for during his six months of incarceration he changed prisons at least three times and eventually landed in solitary confinement at the notorious Butyrki prison, whose cell number 103 he was later to immortalize in a poem entitled "I Love" (1922).

Mayakovsky's stay in prison became a turning point in his life. Although he was also allowed to draw, he must have spent a great deal of time reading serious books and it was then, according to his own testimony, that he wrote his first poetry. He must also have decided that, at least for the time being, the Revolution would have to do without him.

In the meantime the wheels of justice were grinding away. After it developed that there were other charges pending against Mayakovsky in connection with the discovery of a secret printing press, his case came to trial on 9 September. All three defendants were found guilty of being members of the Social Democratic party and of having installed a secret printing press on which they had printed revolutionary material. One was sentenced to six years of hard labor, while the other two, being minors, were committed to the custody of their parents for correction.

## From Revolution to Education

Sixteen-year-old Vladimir found himself at a crossroads. He and everybody who knew him had little doubt that he could do well at whatever he attempted. But while his many other talents were still latent, he had already demonstrated an exceptional talent for drawing. Later he recalled: "I thought to myself: I can't write poetry, my attempts [at Butyrki prison] were pitiful. So I turned to painting" (1:18). He went to study with the painter Stanislav Zhukovsky, at whose studio he painted miniature silver services, but he earned little and soon realized that he was learning less. He then joined the studio of another painter, Petr Kelin, who would also prepare him for the entrance examination to the Moscow Institute for the Study of Painting, Sculpture, and Architecture. Kelin, according to Mayakovsky, was a "realist" who "hated prettiness," and also a good teacher. Mayakovsky was later remembered as a student who tried to develop his own "original" style of drawing and who would talk back to his teacher, who, however, was very fond of him.

Mayakovsky passed his entrance examination in the fall of 1911, after an initial failure. He worked hard at the Institute and certainly would have graduated with honors if poetry and the futurist movement had not entered his life. Even so, he became a competent draftsman and cartoonist.

At the time when Mayakovsky entered the Institute, the world of art was in ferment. Many Russian artists were studying or working in Paris and Munich—where cubism and expressionism were in their early stages—and brought both news and canvasses to Russia. Mayakovsky's first acquaintance with modernism was through painting. Even later, when he had become primarily a poet, it was in the visual arts that he was always *au courant* of the latest trends, for in literature he was hampered by his own monolingualism. Also, Russian poetry was generally more independent of Western tendencies than Russian painting.

It was David Burlyuk (1882–1967) who introduced Mayakovsky not only to modernist painting but also to modernist poetry. Burlyuk, though formally an art student like Mayakovsky, was in fact already a mature painter who had participated in the *Blaue Reiter* exhibition in Munich (1911), considered the start of German expressionism. However, Burlyuk was drawn even more powerfully to the cubism of Picasso and Braque, which had just then reached its "analytic" stage. Burlyuk also wrote poetry, modernist in a rather vague and anarchic way. While he lacked Mayakovsky's flamboyance, Burlyuk was a remarkable man. One-eyed, prematurely obese, untidy in his personal appearance, he was not only a talented and versatile artist, but also a shrewd judge of talent and a capable organizer. He understood the young Mayakovsky better than anyone else and treated him exactly right. Mayakovsky in turn was genuinely fond of Burlyuk, and their cordial relations were in no way affected by Burlyuk's emigration to America after the Revolution.

The crucial events of September 1912 were later described by Mayakovsky in "I Myself":

Concert hall. Rakhmaninov. "The Isle of the Dead."[3] Fled from this unbearable boredom set to music. A moment later Burlyuk followed me. We laughed heartily. Went out for a stroll together. A memorable night. Conversation. From Rakhmaninovian boredom we passed on to our school boredom, from school boredom to classical boredom at large. David's was the anger of a master who has overtaken his contemporaries, mine the pathos of a socialist who knew of the inevitable downfall of all that was old and decrepit. And so Russian futurism was born. Next night. During the day I made a poem. Rather, pieces of one. Bad. Never printed. Night. Sretensky Boulevard. I read the lines to Burlyuk, adding that they were by a friend of mine. David stopped. Looked me over. Roared: "Come on, you've written this yourself! Why, you're a poetic genius!" This grandiose and undeserved epithet made me happy. I went all out for poetry. That night, quite unexpectedly, I became a poet. (1:19–20)

Mayakovsky's account is, of course, a dramatized and compressed version of the actual course of events. Russian futurism was not born on "one memorable night." Though the Russian futurists denied it, the movement almost certainly received its initial stimulus from the Italo-French futurism of Filippo Tommaso Marinetti (1876–1944), whose "First Futurist Manifesto" had appeared in *Le Figaro* (Paris) in 1909. As early as April 1910 a group of poets and painters calling themselves *budetlyane* (from *budet*, "will be," hence "futurists") published a slender volume entitled *Sadok sudey* [A trap for judges]. Among its contributors were David Burlyuk and his brother Nikolay, Vasily Kamensky, and Viktor ("Velimir") Khlebnikov, all of whom were to play a significant role in Russian Futurism.

## The Birth of Futurism

The early futurists called their group Hylaea (in Russian, *Gileya*), after an ancient Greek settlement not far from the home of the Burlyuks in Kherson province, and displayed an archaist and primitivist tendency alien to Mayakovsky and the later futurist mainline. (These tendencies were, however, powerful in Russian modernist art.) The futurist manifestoes in the miscellanies *A Slap in the Face of Public Taste* (December 1912) and *A Trap for Judges,* (February 1913) concentrated on those aspects of modernism also reflected in the poems which Mayakovsky contributed to these collections: urbanism, cubist deformation of imagery, and bold manipulation of language in total disregard of poetic, or even grammatical, conventions.

Mayakovsky—the youngest of the signers of the futurist manifestoes and without any previous published, or exhibited, work to his credit—almost immediately became the central figure of the small group. Burlyuk, a brilliant impresario, chose to take the futurist message to the public not by way of the printed word, but directly. The public appearances of the futurists, which combined poetry reading, lecture, debate, and "happening," were advertised by publicity stunts. Burlyuk would appear in public with a tree branch and a little bird perched on it painted on his cheek; Mayakovsky would wear his famous yellow jacket (sewn for him by his mother); Kamensky—a poet and painter of some talent and also one of Russia's first amateur flyers—might give a flying exhibition. Such antics soon caused Burlyuk and Mayakovsky to be expelled from art school, but it did not matter: futurism had caught the attention of the press and of the public.

When Burlyuk took the show on the road in the winter of 1913, the futurists were preceded by their growing notoriety, and they drew good crowds most of the time. Judging from newspaper reports, from notes and résumés of the participants, including Mayakovsky's, and from reminiscences of people in attendance, the futurist evenings were not only provocative but also entertaining, and even informative. Burlyuk knew modern art as well as anybody and was good at explaining the ideas underlying it. Mayakovsky was the star of the show. As a reader of his own poetry he had only one rival, the "ego-futurist" Igor Severyanin, who traveled with the show for a while but then quarreled with the others and departed. Even more amazing, Mayakovsky, with his eighth-grade education, also lectured challengingly and competently on the aesthetics of futurism before audiences of alert intellectuals. He quickly developed into a superb debater and a master of witty repartee. He was now a well-built six-footer, ruggedly handsome, with a velvety bass voice and a dominant stage presence. Though Mayakovsky may not have liked it, some critics actually saw him as a rather pleasant youth, whose talks were well delivered and made a good deal of sense. Of course there were jeers and insults, too.

After the road show ended, Mayakovsky went on "living on the boulevards" of Moscow, as he put it, yet working hard all the while and rapidly maturing as a poet. In May 1913 he produced a first collection of his own, with the characteristic title of *I*. The end of the same year saw his debut as a dramatist. In the summer Mayakovsky worked on a play which he wanted to call "The Revolt of Things," but eventually titled *Vladimir Mayakovsky: A Tragedy*. It was performed at the Luna Park Theater in St. Petersburg on 2 and 4 December, alternating with the even more notorious *Victory over the Sun* by the futurist Aleksey Kruchonykh, with music by Mikhail Matyushin and sets by Kazimir Malevich. Mayakovsky staged his play himself and played the lead role, that of the poet Vladimir Mayakovsky. The sets were designed by Iosif Shkolnik and the costumes by Pavel Filonov. Little did the audiences, which responded to both pieces mostly with derision, realize that they were face to face with the work of artists who were to occupy important places in the history of world art and world literature. However, the shows played to packed houses, in spite of absurdly high ticket prices. *Vladimir Mayakovsky* was the more successful of the two pieces. It drew some catcalls, but by and large Mayakovsky was able to deliver his emotion-laden monologues to what must have been a dumbfounded audience.

*Vladimir Mayakovsky: A Tragedy* appeared in print in March 1914, by which time Mayakovsky had established himself as the leader of the futurist school, which had become a fixture on the literary scene. Several more almanacs—under such provocative titles as *The Croaked Moon, Mares' Milk,* and *Roaring Parnassus*—appeared, and the first issue of a *First Journal of Russian Futurists* was published in March 1914.

The war which broke out in the summer of 1914 curtailed further publishing activities, but had no serious effect on Mayakovsky. As the only son of a widowed mother he was initially exempt from the draft. Eventually he was drafted, but never performed any real military service, much less front-line duty. Like virtually everyone else, though, he went through a period of patriotic fervor. Mayakovsky's contributions to the Russian war effort—mostly anti-German jingles and cartoons—were, however, less embarrassing than the effusions of such established poets as Valery Bryusov or Vyacheslav Ivanov. They were unpretentious, folksy, and often, after their own fashion, masterful. Who but Mayakovsky could come up with a perfectly good rhyme for "Hohenzollern", the name of Germany's ruling house?

The truly important things in Mayakovsky's life had little to do with the war. In the fall of 1913 he had met Elena ("Elsa") Yurevna Kagan, teenage daughter of a prosperous Moscow lawyer. Elsa liked his company and even his poetry, but treated him "with kindness and indifference," as she later recalled. She eventually became Elsa Triolet (the name of her first husband, her second husband being the writer Louis Aragon), a major French writer, and a lifelong friend. Through her, moreover, Mayakovsky met the great love of his life, Elsa's sister Lilya, two years older than Mayakovsky and married to Osip Maksimovich Brik (1888–1945), a well-to-do lawyer with serious literary interests. Lilya, petite and very pretty in a feline way, was also an extraordinarily clever woman. Mayakovsky's first acquaintance with the Briks in the summer of 1915 was a turning point in his life. Lilya did not love Mayakovsky, but she was willing to tolerate his love for her, give him a home, and act as a restraining and civilizing muse. Osip Maksimovich, who had lost whatever erotic interest he may once have had in his wife, had no objection to a *ménage à trois*. He soon became Mayakovsky's publisher, and eventually his collaborator in a variety of literary ventures, ending as a major literary critic and theorist in his own right. The cultured, worldly-wise, and mature Briks contributed much to the formation of Mayakovsky's whole outlook on life, from his becoming a fastidious dresser to his cosmopolitan view of the world and his impassioned denunciations of anti-Semitism.

The first complete edition of Mayakovsky's first *poema* (the Russian term for a narrative poem several hundred lines long), *A Cloud in Trousers* (1915), bears the dedication "To you, Lilya." It was, however, written for the most part before Mayakovsky had met Lilya Brik. The object of the poet's unrequited love in that poem is named Mariya, and her prototype, if there was one, has not been identified with certainty. But the heroine of his next *poema, The Backbone Flute* (1915), is Lilya, to whom it was also dedicated. Mayakovsky read and discussed *The Backbone Flute* and the poems which followed it with the Briks before their publication.

Like some other poems from the years of Mayakovsky's most intense infatuation with Lilya, *The Backbone Flute* is an accumulation of hyperbolic conceits which give the poet's love, jealousy, and suffering truly gigantic or even cosmic proportions. This may appear mannered and affected, or even smacks of *boutade,* but there is evidence that there was genuine anguish at the bottom of it all and that behind his self-confident facade Mayakovsky was emotionally in a bad way. Maksim Gorky (1868–1936), even then a famous writer, who heard Mayakovsky recite *The Backbone Flute* in the summer of 1915, reports on not only how impressed he was with Mayakovsky's splendid rendition of this and other poems, but also how taken aback he was when Mayakovsky suddenly broke down and began to cry. Mayakovsky later claimed that it was Gorky who broke down and cried, but his sarcastic lines (Gorky's report is quite sympathetic) were written in 1928, by which time the two had quarreled, and Gorky's account is much more credible anyway.

Mayakovsky's reaction to the horrors of war was set down in a rather lengthy *poema, War and the World,* once more dedicated to Lilya. The Russian title, *Voyna i mir,* is the same as that of Tolstoy's great novel, since Russian *mir* means "peace" as well as "world." Of course, the challenge to Russia's greatest writer, who had died only a few years earlier (1910), was only a gesture, for Mayakovsky made no serious attempt to deal with any of Tolstoy's themes. Instead there was an almost grotesquely narcissistic display of the poet's own distress at the sight of so much suffering. Still, the tone of the poem is vigorously strident throughout and its broken staccato rhythms and apocalyptic imagery express genuine anguish and a sincere loathing of the war. Consequently, it had a great deal of trouble with the censors and appeared in full only after the Revolution.

Mayakovsky's last major poem written before the Revolution was *Man* (or *The Man*, or *A Man*, since Russian has neither a definite nor an indefinite article), which also appeared only after the Revolution. The "man" is of course Mayakovsky, again identified by name in the text of the poem, whose subject is once more the poet's cosmic anguish caused by frustrated love. The theme of suicide appears explicitly and persistently. *Man*, like *A Cloud in Trousers* and other pieces of that period, incorporates a wealth of religious imagery, blasphemously distorted and travestied, of course, yet not without an undertone of religious feeling. The poem also contains some of Mayakovsky's most purely lyrical lines.

If Lilya Brik was a lifesaver, the revolution which swept the czar from his throne in February 1917 was another. As Viktor Shklovsky, a leading theorist of the avant-garde, put it, "Mayakovsky entered the Revolution as he would enter his own home." He looked over— quite literally, according to his autobiographic notes—the Provisional Government of Aleksandr Kerensky and decided that it was not nearly revolutionary enough. His 200-line poem "Revolution: A Poetic Chronicle," written in April, made it clear that he saw events up to that point as only a preview of greater things to come. Mayakovsky's autobiographic entry under "October, 1917" says laconically: "Accept or not accept [the Bolshevik Revolutiuon]? There was no such question for me, or for the other Moscow futurists. My Revolution. I went to the Smolny [Lenin's headquarters during the October Revolution]. Worked. All that came along." Apparently, Mayakovsky was an eyewitness of the crucial hours of the *coup d'état*, though only as a bystander. Nothing ever made him prouder than the fact that the red sailors who marched on the Winter Palace to topple the Provisional Government were singing a ditty of his composition: "Bolt your pineapple, stuff your face with quail, / Your last day, bourgeois, has come without fail!"

### The Poet and the Revolution

The October Revolution immediately created a new situation, even on the literary scene. Most periodicals ceased publication, and many established writers and artists left Russia. Clubs and work-shops of proletarian writers and artists soon sprang up all over the country. A shortage of all commodities, including paper, caused a temporary return to oral media, the bulletin board, and the public spectacle. Lenin and the party had more important things to worry about than literature and the arts, which were left to the attention of Anatoly Lunacharsky, himself a critic and playwright, a kindly and generous man who believed in creative freedom—on the grounds that it could only help the Revolution, since truly creative artists could not possibly be reactionaries or counterrevolutionaries.

The Moscow futurists took full advantage of the new situation. Their "Decree No. 1 on the Democratization of Art" proclaimed:

Comrades and citizens, we, the leaders of Russian futurism, the revo-lutionary art of youth, declare: 1. Starting today, with the abolition of the Czar's regime, the *domicile of art* in the closets and sheds of human genius—palaces, galleries, salons, libraries, and theatres—*is abrogated.* 2. In the name of the great march of equality for all, in the field of culture, let the *Free Word* of the creative personality be written on the walls, fences, roofs, and streets of our cities and villages, on the backs of automobiles, carriages, streetcars, and on the clothes of all citizens. 3. Let *pictures,* in color, be flung like colored rainbows across streets and squares, from house to house, delighting and ennobling the eye of the passer-by.

And so on, in the same vein. On Mayday 1918 the walls and fences of Moscow were indeed decorated with futurist and suprematist pictures.

From 1918 to 1921 Mayakovsky found his principal outlet in placards and posters, as well as (after 1919) the display windows of the Soviet telegraph agency (ROSTA), where people could find versified comments, illustrated by cartoons, on current events and issues: the progress of the war, efforts to keep the supply lines open, the struggle against defeatism and sabotage, famine relief, as well as such less momentous topics as the government's effort to stop illegal vodka stills. This voluminous output of purely utilitarian work did not necessarily mean that Mayakovsky had "stepped on

the throat of his own songs" to become a "latrine cleaner" and "bard
of boiled water," as he later put it. In many of these pieces Mayakovsky displayed precisely the same qualities that were the best
part of his "serious" poetry: ingenious rhymes, clever puns, striking
imagery, and spirited whimsy. Besides, primitivism had been a
significant element in avant-garde art and poetry all along.

In those years there existed a widespread notion that the political
triumph of the working class would lead to the birth of a new,
distinctly proletarian culture. The futurists had wanted to "throw
all the classics" overboard even before the Revolution. Now Mayakovsky proclaimed:

> You find a White Guard man—
> you shoot him, don't you?
> But have you forgotten Raphael?
> Have you forgotten Rastrelli?
> ("Too Early to Rejoice," 1918 [2:16])

Characteristically, Francesco Bartolomeo Rastrelli, the eighteenth-
century architect who built the beautiful palaces of St. Petersburg,
was selected for execution for the sake of a pun: *rasstrelyat'* is the
Russian word for "shoot." Raphael was a less fortuitous victim: his
name had been a code word for "pure art" in Russian revolutionary
aesthetics even in the nineteenth century. A few lines later, Mayakovsky also kills off Russia's national poet, Aleksandr Pushkin—
for his name produces another neat pun *(pushka,* "gun," "cannon").
It seemed as though revolutionary ardor and futurist poetics could
coexist. But soon some problems developed. The poets of the proletarian culture *(Proletkult)* movement expressed their revolutionary
message in conventionally versified poems. By 1921, when Mayakovsky issued his "Order No. 2 to the Army of the Arts" ("Order
No. 1" was issued in 1918), he brushed off the *Proletkult* as artistic
reactionaries "who put patches / on Pushkin's faded dresscoat." The
difficulty was that the *Proletkult*—and the party too—wanted politically loyal, "progressive" content, but expressed in a conventional, intelligible form. But this problem caught up with
Mayakovsky only later.

One of the features of what was then believed to be the emergence
of a new, proletarian culture was the mass spectacle, a "happening"
to bring art to the masses. Propaganda trucks and propaganda trains

were a part of this; so were open air theater performances in which
Red Army units and civic groups performed as extras in mass scenes.
On the third anniversary of the October Revolution a crowd of over
a hundred thousand watched a reenactment of the storming of the
Winter Palace by ten thousand participants. Mayakovsky naturally
joined this trend. His play *Mystery-Bouffe: A Heroic, Epic, and Satirical Representation of Our Epoch* was presented at the Petrograd
Musical Theater to celebrate the first anniversary of the October
Revolution. It was staged by the great Vsevolod Meyerhold (1874–
1942), even then a famous director, with amateur actors. Mayakovsky played one major and two minor roles himself. Subsequent
performances in 1920 and 1921 developed the idea of a "happening"
even more. Both productions were filled with acrobatics and circus
tricks. The 1921 presentation was actually done in a circus and
employed 350 actors and dancers, who performed (in German!)
before the delegates of the Third Congress of the Comintern.

While Mayakovsky maintained his bohemian life-style and was
as active a habitué of Moscow literary cafés as he had been before
the war, his life now acquired another dimension. More and more
often he was invited to lecture and read his poetry before audiences
of soldiers, workers, Communist party members, etc. As if this
were not enough, he developed yet another line of work in 1918.
He had always been interested in film and now, after establishing
contact with the "Neptune" film studio, he wrote several scenarios
and also played the lead in some films. His first and most successful
film scenario, *Not for Money Born* (March 1918), was based on Jack
London's novel *Martin Eden* and deals with the career of a writer of
genius who can handle adversity well, but eventually falls victim
to success. Naturally Mayakovsky played the lead and of course he
played himself, as he always did. The film ran for several years all
over the Soviet Union. His next film, *The Lady and the Hooligan,*
also seems to have been a success. In 1927, when Mayakovsky
published a collection of his film scenarios, he wrote in his preface:
"My second and third scenarios were sentimental nonsense made to
order. . . . Nonsense not because it was worse than other films,
but because it wasn't any better." (12:126).

Mayakovsky was more pleased with a scenario entitled *Fettered by
Film,* in which the technical possibilities inherent in silent film—
montage in particular—were exploited rather cleverly. Mayakovsky
played the lead (this time a painter), with Lilya Brik as his leading

lady. He also drew the poster advertising the film. It showed Lilya Brik's bust, strangely emaciated and with no breasts, growing from a giant heart, her thin arms fettered by a snakelike roll of film.

Mayakovsky's preoccupation with film did not last long. Early in 1919 he was at work on a major epic poem, *150,000,000*. He was also busy doing political, martial, civic, didactic, sanitary, and other jingles for the show windows of ROSTA.

*150,000,000* (1920–21), like *Mystery-Bouffe,* was an effort to fuse art and political propaganda. With much wit and invention, but a great deal of bombast and grotesquerie too, it is an allegory of the decisive battle between 150,000,000 Soviet workers and the evil forces of capitalism, led by Woodrow Wilson. In retrospect, *150,000,000* seems an example of avant-gárde art at its best, but it brought Mayakovsky little joy. To begin with, he had considerable trouble getting it published by Gosizdat, the state publishing house (private publishers still existed in the Soviet Union at the time). Apparently Lunacharsky's personal intervention finally caused reluctant Gosizdat officials to publish it—in 5,000 copies, which was a lot in 1921, with paper still scarce. Reactions were generally negative. Readers who judged it on artistic grounds—Boris Pasternak, for example—saw it as the product of talent wasted on clumsy propaganda. Those who judged it on political grounds found it preposterously grandiloquent, unmindful of political realities, and unworthy of its reader—who knew very well that Woodrow Wilson was not enormously fat, but very thin, and that Chicago was not on the Atlantic ocean. Of course Mayakovsky knew these things too. A memorandum by Lenin himself, addressed to Lunacharsky on 6 May 1921, read:

> Aren't you ashamed to support the printing of 5,000 copies of Mayakovsky's *150,000,000?*
> This thing is absurd, stupid, monstrously stupid, and pretentious. In my opinion only one in ten of such pieces should be printed, and no more than 1,500 copies for libraries and eccentrics.
> And Lunacharsky ought to be whipped for futurism.

On the reverse side of the memorandum, there is Lunacharsky's reply: "I did not particularly like the piece, but (1) such an eminent poet as Bryusov was enthusiastic and asked for 20,000 copies to be printed; (2) when read by the author himself, the piece was clearly successful, and with workers at that."

Valery Bryusov, by the way, had been a favorite whipping boy of the futurists in the days of "A Slap in the Face of Public Taste," but he was an excellent judge of talent. Ironically, this poem, perhaps Mayakovsky's best purely "Soviet" effort, to this day receives no more than lukewarm praise in the Soviet Union. It is said to be somewhat "immature" and not yet fully on the level of Mayakovsky's later communist classics, such as *Vladimir Ilich Lenin*. Such is the power of a casual remark by Lenin, who, wiser than the scholars and critics who defer to his judgment, stressed that his was "strictly a layman's" opinion.

The year 1921 was the last one of war and civil war. In 1921, too, "war communism" was officially terminated and replaced by the New Economic Policy (NEP), which made substantial concessions to free enterprise in agriculture, trade, and light industry. The NEP was an economic success, but ideologically it was a heavy blow to true communist believers. Mayakovsky followed the party line by satirizing the greedy *nepman* and the abuses of private enterprise without, however, criticizing the basic policy. Incidentally, Mayakovsky, unlike some other communists, had no ascetic aversion to bourgeois comfort. He wore a three-piece suit, a clean shirt and a tie, and was always clean shaven at a time when many of his confreres were still sporting odd pieces of civil war uniforms, dirty boots, and unshaven faces. He also discovered that his skill as a rhymester and cartoonist was quite marketable in the budding Soviet economy. Mayakovsky's jingles and posters were soon selling anything from galoshes to cigarettes. In fact, he even designed properly educational candy wrappers.

The years 1921 and 1922 also witnessed an amazingly rapid transition to political and administrative stability with the installation of a powerful new bureaucracy. Mayakovsky immediately took up the challenge and dedicated his remaining years, to a considerable extent, to a struggle against Soviet philistinism, the rebirth of petit-bourgeois morality and tastes, and the rapidly ossifying Soviet bureaucracy. Of course, Mayakovsky's spirited, and sometimes heavyhanded, sorties were made with the full approval of the party and its affiliated organizations. Many of them appeared in *Izvestiya* [News], organ of the Soviet government, and *Komsomolskaya pravda* [Comsomol truth], organ of the Young Communist League.

In order to remain in the mainstream of Soviet journalism, Mayakovsky had to jettison some of his futurist baggage, adopting a less

challenging imagery and simpler language. This step was eased by
the fact that the entire poetic establishment of which Mayakovsky
had been a part had dissolved by 1922. David Burlyuk emigrated
to the United States. Velimir Khlebnikov, the only poet of Mayakovsky's stature among the futurists, died in 1922. Boris Pasternak,
who scored a huge success with his collection *Life My Sister* in 1922,
did not approve of the tendency of Mayakovsky's poetry, and the
two poets became almost wholly alienated from each other. Aleksandr Blok, surely the greatest poet among Mayakovsky's contemporaries, died in 1921, the same year Nikolay Gumilev, leader of
the Acmeist school, was shot as a counterrevolutionary. Acmeism
as a school ceased to exist, though Anna Akhmatova and Osip
Mandelshtam, its most gifted members, were yet to write some of
their best work. As for futurism, Valery Bryusov, then deputy
director of the Department of Literature in the People's Commissariat of Education, wrote in the September–October 1922 issue of
the journal *Pechat' i revolutsiya* [Printed word and revolution]: "The
basic task of Futurism was to put into action the principle that
language, as the material of poetry, is subject to manipulation by
the poet. Futurism has realized this principle in theory as well as
in practice, and with that its role in Russian literature may be
regarded as completed." Although Mayakovsky doggedly stuck to
his futurist loyalties and even organized a publishing company bearing the name "Moscow Association of Futurists" (MAF) in 1922,
Bryusov was right. Mayakovsky's own work was losing more and
more of its futurist elements.

## Mayakovsky and the World

In May 1922 Mayakovsky made his first trip abroad, to Riga,
capital of the recently established Republic of Latvia. Then as now,
Riga had a large Russian population, and Mayakovsky planned to
give a public lecture. His political views were so well known,
however, that the local chief of police refused permission. After all,
only a couple of years earlier Latvia had barely escaped becoming a
Soviet republic. Mayakovsky retaliated with a vicious verse satire
in which he lampooned every aspect of life in the young republic.
It shows Mayakovsky the world traveler at his worst. He never
pretended to be objective and insisted on seeing things through the
eyes of a Soviet propagandist. But he was not always so recklessly

mindless of the truth or so hostile as he was here, speaking of a neighboring country which the Soviet Union had, after all, officially recognized.

Later in 1922 Mayakovsky visited western Europe for the first time. His first stop was Berlin, where he spent most of October and November. Relations between the U.S.S.R. and the Weimar Republic were relatively good throughout the 1920s, and Mayakovsky's references to Germany and the Germans decidedly follow the official line. Also, Russia, one of the losers in the war, felt a certain solidarity with Germany, another loser, and shared a common hostility toward the Allies. Finally, there was a strong Communist party in Germany and many German intellectuals were oriented toward the left. Germany also had a talented, active, and largely leftist avant-garde, so that Mayakovsky could fully sympathize with the art of Georg Grosz and Otto Dix. And so Mayakovsky made a series of public appearances in Germany without incident. From Berlin Mayakovsky went to Paris, where he stayed for ten action packed days.

With Elsa Triolet acting as his guide and interpreter, he met some French writers (he wanted to see Henri Barbusse and Anatole France, but they were out of town and the best he could get was Jean Cocteau), attended the funeral of Marcel Proust, and saw a great deal of French painting. He visited the fall salon and a number of other galleries, and met Picasso, Braque, Delaunay, and Léger at their ateliers.

Upon his return to Moscow on 13 December, Mayakovsky immediately began giving public lectures on his travel impressions and published a series of sketches on life in Berlin and Paris, as well as a fairly detailed survey of contemporary French painting, the latter a knowledgeable, though slanted, piece of art criticism. Mayakovsky the art critic is still very much the futurist. When he finds fault with modern painting, it is not on account of its extravagance or anarchy, but rather for a tendency, which he thinks he has detected, toward "academism" and "pleasing the bourgeois public" (he singles out Braque in this connection). Mayakovsky's aesthetic is still that of futurism when he praises Léger (his favorite) for his "realism." Clearly Mayakovsky's notion of "realism" is not the conventional mimetic one, but is based on the principle that the artist should be true to the nature of his material: "I am struck by Léger's matter-of-fact treatment of paint not as means of transmitting some sort of space, or such, but as the material which colors objects" (4:248).

Upon his return from the West, Mayakovsky took up two of the most important projects of his life: the avant-garde journal *Left Front* (or *Lef*) and his finest long poem, *About That,* to appear in the first issue of *Lef,* which came out in March 1923. Mayakovsky's application for permission to start his journal, addressed to the propaganda department *(Agit-otdel)* of the Central Committee of the Communist party in early January, specified these goals for the journal:

(a) To advance the finding of a communist way for every art form; (b) to revise the ideology and practice of so-called left art, freeing it of individualist antics and developing its communist aspects; (c) to conduct a stubborn campaign among the applied arts to make them accept the communist way and ideology; (d) by accepting the most revolutionary trends in the field of art, to serve as an avant-garde for Russian and world art; (e) to acquaint the Russian working-class public with the achievements of European art, but not in the person of its canonized official representatives, but in the person of their literary and artistic youth, now rejected by the European bourgeoisie, yet representing the young shoots of a new proletarian culture; (f) to combat in all possible ways all seekers of compromise in the field of art, who substitute old and worn phrases about absolute values and eternal beauty for communist ideology; (g) to produce examples of literary and artistic creation serving not the satisfaction of aesthetic tastes, but the demonstration of creative devices suited to the production of effective propaganda pieces; (h) to combat decadence, aesthetic mysticism, self-contained formalism, and indifferent naturalism and support tendentious realism based on the utilization of the technical devices of all revolutionary schools in art (13:204).

This statement contains details suggesting a retreat from Mayakovsky's earlier, purely futurist positions. "Freeing art of individualist antics" could be applied to such works of his own as *Mystery-Bouffe* and *150,000,000.* The inclusion of "self-contained formalism" among trends to be combated was equally significant. The Russian formalist school of critics and scholars, gathered around OPOYAZ (acronym for the "Society for the Study of Poetic Language") since 1914, had been intimately linked to the futurist movement. Some of the formalists, such as Viktor Shklovsky and Roman Jakobson, were Mayakovsky's personal friends. The formalists' view of "art as device" was in full accord with the futurist aesthetic, and Mayakovsky never abandoned this notion. But its inevitable corollary—the formalist demand that a work of art be treated independently of the artist's biography, and the history of art and literature separately from social and political history—was now rejected by the spokesman of *Lef*. A strictly utilitarian conception of art was always maintained by *Lef*, and particularly by Osip Brik, its main theoretician. As if to advertise this attitude, *Lef* concluded a written agreement with the Moscow Association of Proletarian Writers (MAPP, later to expand into the Russian Association of Proletarian Writers, RAPP), pledging mutual cooperation in "steadfastly unmasking bourgeois-aristocratic and pseudo-cooperative literary groups" and promoting the "awareness of readership for the communist goals of the proletariat."

However, the content of *Lef* during its two years of existence (seven issues appeared, the last in June 1925) hardly matched the doctrinaire program that launched it on its way. It featured poetry by Pasternak, Vasily Kamensky, Nikolay Aseev, Aleksey Kruchonykh, and Velimir Khlebnikov (posthumously), prose fiction by Isaak Babel, and theoretical essays by Shklovsky and Brik. There were many illustrated contributions by artists, directors, and filmmakers, such as Vsevolod Meyerhold, Dziga Vertov, Sergey Eisenstein, and Rodchenko. And last but not least, the first issue of *Lef* contained Mayakovsky's greatest lyric *poema*—an admitted love poem, yet!—*About That*.

*About That* (where "that" is, of course, "love") is once again an allegoric outpouring of the love and suffering of Vladimir Mayakovsky. The object of his love is still Lilya, here identified even by her real telephone number. His love is, as always, frustrated in a kaleidoscopic sequence of surrealist visions. There is no positive social message, except for, at the very end of the poem, a utopian dream of a world in which "no one will have to beg and plead for love, / but that on your first cry, 'Comrade!' / the whole Earth will turn to you."

It must be remembered that Mayakovsky, while writing *About That*, continued to produce propaganda verse at a furious pace. While indulging in lyric effusions of cosmic love, he was also turning out freewheeling antireligious propaganda, superb commercial jingles, or yet another ballad on the evils of homemade vodka.

On 21 January 1924 Lenin died. Though it is difficult to assess a leader's true popularity in a totalitarian state, there seems to have been much genuine grief at his passing. Mayakovsky, who personally had no real reason to be devoted to Lenin, appears to have grieved sincerely. Most of that year he worked on what is officially considered his *chef d'oeuvre*, a 3,000-line *poema* entitled *Vladimir Ilich Lenin*. In 1924 Mayakovsky traveled extensively throughout the Soviet Union, giving lectures and reading his poetry, including excerpts from *Vladimir Ilich Lenin*. Thus fragments of the poem appeared in various journals and newspapers at various locations, before the full first part (lines 1–922) appeared in Mayakovsky's own *Lef* in January 1925. The whole poem appeared as a separate booklet later in 1925. *Vladimir Ilich Lenin* is the communist equivalent of a religious epic, mixing the didactic, the panegyric, and the devotional. It tells of the historical development of capitalism and socialism, the ascendancy of the working class, Lenin's wise and heroic leadership of the Revolution, the first steps toward a new society in the U.S.S.R., the shock of the beloved leader's death, and the universal grief at his funeral.

For Mayakovsky 1924 was the beginning of a heady period of success. His posters, cartoons, and jingles (he was still doing commercials, too), and especially his innumerable public appearances throughout the Soviet Union, had made him a public figure. Though he had many literary enemies, he was now clearly in the good graces of the party: the frequent trips he was allowed to take abroad at government expense were evidence of that. Also, the Left Art aesthetic which he championed was now, for a few brief years, genuinely in vogue, finding ample expression on the stage, in film and photography, and in literature. Only in painting was the heyday of Russian modernism already over, thanks to emigration (Larionov, Goncharova, Chagall, Kandinsky, David Burlyuk), or death (Popova, Rozanova, Vladimir Burlyuk). For a few years constructivism, factography, biomechanics, and other such fashions were paraded as "Soviet" achievements. Mayakovsky's line "Time, forward march!" seemed a perfect slogan, not only for a society on the march into a new age, but also for an art that would contribute to the transition to a life made easy and beautiful by machines and rational organization.

## Mayakovsky the Traveler

In 1924 the idea of the World Revolution was still alive, and Mayakovsky believed in it. Hence he had good ideological reason to travel often to the West. On 23 October 1924 the commissar of public education, still A. V. Lunacharsky, wrote to the appropriate department of the Council of the National Economy: "The poet Mayakovsky is going abroad as a correspondent and to do research. The Commissariat of Public Education requests that he be allowed to retain his room (3 Lubyansky Prospect, apt. 12) for the time of his absence, as his works and manuscripts are located there." This document illuminates the situation of that time very well indeed. There was a terrible housing shortage in Moscow then, much worse than today. Mayakovsky, one of the privileged few, not only had a room of his own (in addition to the Briks' apartment, where he actually lived), but could keep it as storage space during his absence. The fact that Lunacharsky, an official of cabinet rank, intervened on his behalf, shows that this was no trivial matter and that Mayakovsky was very much in the good graces of the party.

On 24 October Mayakovsky departed for Paris, where he intended to request a visa to go on to the United States. Failing to obtain it, he stayed in Paris to be present at the entombment of Jean Jaurès in the Pantheon (duly celebrated in a poem) and at the solemn raising of the red flag over the building of the Soviet embassy on 14 December (also celebrated in a poem, "The Flag"). After his return to Moscow on 27 December Mayakovsky immediately immersed himself in his manifold public activities, writing his usual amount of utilitarian poetry and prose, addressing various audiences, participating in discussion meetings and committee work, etc. Mayakovsky took a genuine interest in the work of others, was kind and considerate to friends, would pick up the gauntlet even of decidedly mediocre opponents, and played his role as a celebrity with unselfconscious charm.

Mayakovsky wished very much to show that his trip to Paris had been important and fruitful. He became an active member of a committee seeing to the preparation of a Soviet pavilion at the International Exhibition of Industrial Arts to be held in Paris in 1925, and by May of that year he had delivered to *Moskovskii rabochii* [The Moscow worker] a cycle of poems entitled *Paris* which combined some genuine Parisian atmosphere with an aggressive anti-capitalist and antibourgeois message.

On 25 May 1925 Mayakovsky was once more on his way to Paris, this time by airplane (needless to say, he loved flying). On 4 June he attended the opening of the Soviet pavilion at the Exhibition of Industrial Arts. His own commercial advertising posters were awarded a silver medal there. He was getting ready to continue on to America, when disaster struck: a thief stole his wallet with all his money. Fortunately the Soviet trade mission advanced him the amount he needed for his journey, on condition that it would be repaid by the State Publishing House by the end of the year. On 20 June Maya-kovsky embarked on the passenger liner *Espagne* from St. Nazaire. The voyage to Vera Cruz, Mexico, with stops in the Azores and Havana, was uneventful. Mayakovsky had ample time both to observe his fellow passengers and to turn his observations into verse. Six nuns traveling together were an easy target for another antire-ligious satire, for instance. A day in Havana confirmed Mayakovsky's notion that the countries of Latin America were colonies of United States capitalism:

One side of it is very exotic. Against the background of a green sea, a black Negro in white trousers is selling a crimson fish, lifting it high over his head by its tail. The other side are the worldwide tobacco and sugar companies which employ tens of thousands of Negro, Spanish, and Russian [!?] laborers. And at the focus of all this wealth there is the American club, ten-storied Ford, Clay and Buck, the first sign of United States domination over all three Americas: North, South, and Central" (*My Discovery of America*. 1926 [7:270])

A day's sightseeing in Havana also produced "Black and White," Mayakovsky's contribution to the struggle against racial discrimination.

Upon arriving in Vera Cruz on 8 July Mayakovsky immediately proceeded by train to Mexico City. For once, he was impressed by the natural landscape, and by cactuses in particular, as is evidenced by a vivid description of sunrise on the train in *My Discovery of America*. Mayakovsky spent more time in Mexico City than he planned, as he was trying to get a visa to the United States, which took time. He stayed at the Soviet embassy, met some Mexican communists, and went sightseeing. He found the Mexican painter Diego Rivera congenial not only as a former cubist and now a modernist painter reaching back to a primitive native tradition, but also as a fellow communist. Mayakovsky was also impressed by Rivera's reputation as a marksman.

Mayakovsky finally received his visa. He was somewhat paranoid about what he felt was an unusual interest taken in his case by the United States immigration authorities. He gave "artist-painter" as his occupation, and said the purpose of his visit was "to exhibit my work." He also deleted from his poetry in progress all politically incriminating lines, such as his suggestion to Willie, the Havana street sweeper, to address his grievances "to Moscow, the Comintern" ("Black and White" [7:23]). Anyway, on 27 July, after having been detained at Laredo for some eight hours ("behind bars," as he later related, not without satisfaction), he was admitted to the United States on a six months visitor's visa upon posting a $500 bond.

Mayakovsky arrived in New York on 31 July. He immediately called his old friend David Burlyuk and soon felt at home. The America Mayakovsky saw in 1925—New York, Cleveland, Detroit, Chicago, Pittsburgh, and Philadelphia—was not mainstream, middle-class WASP America, but The America of "ethnic" neighborhoods, with viable ethnic organizations, newspapers, theaters, etc. There had been an influx of millions of immigrants who spoke or understood Russian in the years just before World War I, and a significant part of them were sympathetic to the communist revolution in Russia. There were more than a few left-wing organizations vigorously active, especially in New York. And so the personal appearances of "the famous proletarian poet," as Mayakovsky was called in the *Daily Worker* and in the left-wing Russian and Jewish press, filled large lecture halls and theaters. There were seven such appearances in New York, two each in Chicago, Detroit, and Philadelphia, and one each in Pittsburgh and Cleveland. Mayakovsky also spent some time and gave several readings at "Nit gedajge," a Jewish workers' summer camp on the Hudson River, and "Nit gedajge" became the title of one of Mayakovsky's finest poems. Mayakovsky also gave a number of newspaper interviews, attended many social functions, and did a lot of sightseeing: Coney Island, a World Series baseball game, the Ford plant in Detroit, the Chicago stockyards. He took notes furiously, immediately translating some of his impressions into poems of his *America* cycle, which includes several of his best pieces. Some of these poems he even read to

American audiences, whose reactions he sometimes incorporated in the poem's final version. Thus "Brooklyn Bridge," otherwise a eulogy to the miracle of American technology, has a jarring dissonance toward the end: "This is where / jobless working men / flung themselves / headlong / into the Hudson River" (7:86–87) (he mistook the East River for the Hudson). The poet related that he owed this line to some people in his American audiences who had pointed out to him that his poem was too positive.

Mayakovsky left America on 28 October, sailing on the *Rochambeau* for Le Havre. His impressions and opinions of America, as expressed in his *America* cycle and in his prose travelogue *My Discovery of America* may be divided into two categories. What he saw with his own eyes and grasped with his own keen intelligence could be marvellously perceptive—his descriptions of the streets of Manhattan, for example. But since he knew no English, he had to rely largely on interpreters who, being communists or communist sympathizers, were very negative about American capitalist society. Hence Mayakovsky's opinions not based on immediate observation are a rehash of familiar leftist clichés.

Mayakovsky's three months in the United States were a success. His visit was a "shot in the arm" to the American Workers party— even financially, for Mayakovsky gave fifty percent of the proceeds from his public appearances to the Russian communist paper *Novy mir* [New world] and the Jewish communist paper *Frajhajt* [Freedom]. The editor of the latter, Schachno Epstein, later reported that Mayakovsky's tour had provided a great moral boost to the revolutionary faction of the New York Garment Workers Union in its struggle against their "do-nothing union bosses." Once, Epstein relates, Mayakovsky spent a whole day on the picket lines with the garment workers.[4] Moreover, the trip to America engendered some truly excellent poetry and prose. In a way it helped to bring Mayakovsky back to world literature after years of narrowly provincial *agit-prop* work. Finally, Mayakovsky apparently had a lot of fun in America and really liked the country and its people. He liked the Negro cabarets in Harlem. He liked to shoot pool on Fourteenth Street. He liked skyscrapers, automobiles, advertising, Broadway. He disliked America's awkward efforts to cultivate her European heritage, the mawkish ornaments stuck on those magnificent skyscrapers, and the small-town morality which accompanied the technical excellence of American films.

## The Return to Soviet Reality

On his way home Mayakovsky began his oft-quoted programmatic poem "Homeward Bound," in which he reassured himself and his readers of his unwavering loyalty to communism. Its concluding lines, written upon his return to Moscow, refer to a "State of the Union" type speech given by Stalin at the fourteenth congress of the Russian Communist party on 18 December 1925. On the next day Mayakovsky read it to an audience at the Moscow Polytechnic Museum. In the poem, Mayakovsky wrote that he wanted "the commissar of Time / to breathe down his neck / with his orders." Even more significantly, he added that he wanted "that together with pig iron / and steel production / the making of verse / be reported on / at the Party congress / by Stalin" (7:94).

The lines on the "commissar of Time" incorporate one of Mayakovsky's most stubborn fixations, one shared with the society whose spokesman he tried to be: that is the notion that history should be made according to plan, rather than allowed to happen. Moreover, his mention of Stalin in a major poem at this early date may have been a lucky accident that assured Mayakovsky's place in Russian literature, though there is a good chance that it was due mainly to the fact that "Stalin" rhymed with *stali,* "steel."

On 27 December 1925 the poet Sergey Esenin committed suicide. He slashed his wrists and wrote his last poem in his own blood ending it with the lines: "In this life, to die is not so new, / But then, to live isn't any newer." He then hanged himself. Esenin— two years younger than Mayakovsky, handsome, blond and blue-eyed—had made a meteoric career. He had little formal education, but he was not the naive peasant lad he pretended to be. He wrote poetry in the style of the city folk-song—maudlin but catchy, and very melodious. It perfectly expresses a Russian's mood when he is crying into his glass, and was then, as it is now, immensely popular in Russia. Esenin's messy suicide had to make people wonder why he took his life. He was, after all, of the people, and it was an embarrassment that a poet of the people had killed himself in the republic of the people. Mayakovsky saw Esenin's suicide as a challenge and responded with his famous poem "To Sergey Esenin" (1926), whose genesis he described in his equally famous essay "How to Make Verse" (1926). The message of the poem, meant as a refutation of Esenin's nihilist despair, turned out to be a gloomy one. Critics had theorized that Esenin fell victim to isolation from his class, that belonging to a collective of class conscious and disciplined writers would have kept him on the right track. Mayakovsky suggests that while those class-conscious comrades might have saved the poet from drink (Esenin was an alcoholic), he would have in that case committed suicide even earlier—from boredom. Mayakovsky finds the tearfully sentimental cult of the poet's memory even worse. He does not care much for Esenin's style, but respects him as "a journeyman of the Russian word," one who will be missed. The poem concludes with a variation on Esenin's last lines: "Our planet / is poorly fitted / for joy. // One must / extract / joy / from days to come. // In this life, / to die / is not so difficult, // to make life / is considerably more difficult" (7:105). Such a grim assessment of the condition of the world is hardly in accord with the task Mayakovsky had set himself:

Aim: in a thoughtful manner, neutralize the impact of Esenin's last poem, make Esenin's end seem uninspiring; put forward another kind of beauty in place of the easy beauty of death, because much energy is needed on the part of working humanity to complete the revolution now begun, and though the road may be difficult, and the contradictions inherent in life under the NEP depressing, it is necessary that we praise the joy of life, the excitement of our arduous march toward communism. ("How to Make Verse" [12:97]).

The year 1926 was a time of intense work and little fun for Mayakovsky. He traveled extensively, often appearing before several groups in a single day. He did not travel in comfort. Trains were slow and rarely had sleeping cars. Hotel rooms, if available, were often dirty and infested with bedbugs. Mayakovsky, a fastidious hypochondriac who feared germs, bore it all with reasonably good humor. There were also hostile local authorities, poor organization, lethargic audiences, and stupid heckling. But Mayakovsky loved the contact with the masses, the free-wheeling discussions in which he always got the better of his hecklers, "wise guys," purists, pedants, and just plain ignoramuses, and the meetings with young poets and writers in the provinces. He also discovered that he could sell a lot of his books at or through personal appearances. It had worked in America, and now it worked in Russia.

Mayakovsky was also trying to get *Lef* started again. His proposal stated that *New Lef* "would continue the work begun by *Art of the*

*Commune* in 1918–19 and *Lef* in 1923–24 by employing art in the building of socialism while seeking a maximal increase in the quality of this art." *New Lef* began publication in January 1927.

In 1926 Mayakovsky also had trouble with the tax inspector, who argued that, for tax purposes, Mayakovsky should be classified as a *kustar'*, the term for an artisan working alone—tolerated but not encouraged by the NEP. Since the work of a *kustar'* was not thought to be of great social value, he was heavily taxed. Mayakovsky maintained that, while he was working by himself, his work greatly benefited society. To drive home his point, Mayakovsky wrote a poem, "Conversation with a Tax Collector about Poetry" (1926); but he also addressed a detailed declaration to the Moscow Department of Taxation asking that his occupation be changed to "worker." He met with some success, but he was in arrears with his taxes until the end of his life. He needed money. He signed contracts with Gosizdat to deliver a comedy and a novel, but neither was ever finished, and the novel may not have been even started. He also did some books for children (with his own drawings) as well as an occasional film scenario or commercial, and his voice could be heard more and more often on the Soviet radio.

In 1927 the Soviet Union celebrated the tenth anniversary of its existence with considerable pride. The regime had not only survived, but had brought Russia to a condition approaching normalcy. Production was returning to prewar levels and the government was preparing to launch its first Five-Year Plan to push the country along the road of rapid industrialization. Mayakovsky was certainly ready to celebrate. He was working on film and stage scenarios, a major poem (*Good: A Poem of the October Revolution*), and a variety of minor pieces, all dedicated to the anniversary. But on the other hand it was becoming clear that many of the ideals and dreams of the Revolution were being abandoned, and that there was a tendency, even among the younger generation, to search for order, stability, and security rather than the excitement of new achievement. In literature, in the visual arts, in film, and in the theater the time of experimentation and bold innovation was over, and a general retreat to premodernist "realist" positions had begun. It was from these positions that Mayakovsky was now being relentlessly attacked, especially by Aleksandr Voronsky and Zakhar Lezhnev, critics of the *Pereval* (Mountain Pass) group. Their thesis, driven home with conviction and force, was that Mayakovsky was a hack writer of "odes," whose mannerist bombast was unworthy of the new Soviet society and its leader, the victorious proletariat. These critics called for more concern with human problems, more sincerity, and more realism. Along with this charge from the right, there came accusations from Leopold Auerbach and other critics of the RAPP group, the extreme left, who berated him for insufficient discipline and class consciousness, and for his "harmful, muddled ideology," insinuating that Mayakovsky was not a true proletarian and his *Lef* a clique of bourgeois bohemians turned fellow travelers.

This new situation was reflected in Mayakovsky's relationship with Maksim Gorky, who had left the Soviet Union in 1921— though without breaking with the regime—and was now living in his villa at Sorrento, Italy. It seemed perfectly in order that the first issue of *New Lef,* which appeared in January 1927, should feature a lengthy and vitriolic poem entitled "A Letter from the Writer Vladimir Vladimirovich Mayakovsky to the Writer Aleksey Maksimovich Gorky." The poem was occasioned by a controversy, then still in progress, over *Tsement* [Cement, 1925], a novel by Gorky's protégé Fedor Gladkov. The book describes a simple Soviet worker, Gleb Chumalov, who brings a giant cement plant, destroyed in the war, back into production while overcoming a host of seemingly insurmountable difficulties. *Cement* and Gorky's own *Mat'*, [Mother, 1907] were the prototypes of what would shortly emerge as the "socialist realist novel." Gorky had spoken approvingly of *Cement,* and it was warmly received by most Soviet critics. *Cement* also sold well, quite possibly because it contained its fair share of raw sex and violence (expunged from later editions). The critics of *Lef* were almost alone in reacting unfavorably to it. Osip Brik saw a contradiction in terms between Gleb Chumalov, the "Soviet Hercules," a character of mythic proportions, and Gladkov's awkward efforts to motivate the action of his novel psychologically.

In his "Letter to Gorky," Mayakovsky spoke once again of the matter: "They sell *Cement* / at every stall. / You, / so it seems, think that such book has value. / There's no cement to be had anywhere, / though Gladkov / has written us / a mass of thanksgiving about cement. / What can I do? Stop up my nostrils, / wrinkling my nose, / till I have passed / that rather longish swamp" (7:207). Mayakovsky then goes on to identify that which many have called "healthy realism" as the "adaptability" and "fawning" of lickspittles.

Only *Lef* and its friends are honest builders of socialism, he says, so why will not Gorky return to the Soviet Union and join them? It might have seemed that Mayakovsky's position was unassailable, but that turned out not to be the case. In 1928 Gorky returned to the Soviet Union for a visit and received a triumphant welcome. In 1931 he returned to the Soviet Union for good, assuming the unchallenged position of the dean of Soviet letters. His blend of conventional realism and revolutionary zeal won out over the uncompromising avant-gardism of *Lef*. But in 1927 Mayakovsky and *Lef* were still confident of the eventual victory of their cause. That year's trip to the West confirmed Mayakovsky's belief that the Soviet government was on his side, and he viewed himself more or less as an official representative of his country. In Warsaw, he was received by an official of the Foreign Ministry. When he visited, the Soviet embassy gave banquets in his honor, inviting local as well as foreign writers, journalists, and celebrities. When interviewed, he spoke for Soviet literature at large. In an interview in the Paris *Journal littéraire,* Mayakovsky chided the French for their ignorance of the new Russian literature: "What do they [the French] know: Tolstoy, Dostoevsky, Gorky. We in Russia have not stopped at Victor Hugo. To us, Dostoevsky is the past. And besides, a good new literature is growing in our country now, as well as a new generation of poets and prose writers."

## The Mobilization of Literature

The first Five-Year Plan began in 1928. Giant industrial projects sprang up all over the country, some in wilderness areas. After the Five-Year Plan had begun auspiciously under Stalin's energetic leadership, the party embarked upon an even more ambitious plan: the collectivization of agriculture, designed to convert Russia's small privately owned farms into a network of mechanized state and collective farms. While the Five-Year Plan produced a viable and expanding heavy industry, the collectivization of agriculture, begun in 1929, was a disaster, causing a heavy drop in agricultural production. A "revolution from above," it necessitated the arrest and deportation of millions of *kulaks* (well-to-do-farmers) and in some instances mass executions of recalcitrant peasants.

For the first time, the party systematically mobilized literature and the arts to support its policies. Scores of writers were dispatched to production and building sites, to newly organized collective farms, or to recently founded schools and institutes, and asked to describe their experiences in a properly edifying manner. Positive as well as negative examples were to be pointed out, with typical phenomena in proper focus. Shortcomings were to be exposed, remedies suggested. The leadership of the party was to be stressed. Success as well as failure was to be attributed to the class factor: wherever shoddy workmanship, lack of labor discipline, or even outright sabotage raised their heads, former capitalists, *kulaks,* or White Guard officers were to be found to be the culprits. The conquering heroes and heroines were to be proletarians, with peasants and intellectuals in the middle, capable of going either way.

No Soviet author was more prepared than Mayakovsky to embrace the mood and the ideology of the Five-Year Plan—and of collectivization as well. No slogan could have been more congenial to him than "The Five Year Plan in Four Years!" It was no accident that the most popular "production" novel of the Five-Year Plan period, Valentin Kataev's *Vremya vpered!* [Time, forward March! 1932], took as its title a quote from Mayakovsky.

Many of Mayakovsky's poems of those years address specific issues and incidents which were also discussed in the Soviet press. He made a point of visiting the building sites of huge new plants and housing projects in the Urals. He proudly partook—poetically, that is—of the joy of one Ivan Kozyrev, a foundry worker of Sverdlovsk in the Urals, whose new apartment featured a bathroom with hot and cold running water. He wrote poetry exhorting the citizenry to sign up for "industrialization bonds." In one of these poems the promise is made that the automobile factories to be built from this money will soon produce "automobiles, / to be paid in installments, and cheap."

The dream of a private automobile would not soon be realized for most Soviet citizens, but in 1928 Mayakovsky became the proud owner of a brand new Renault, brought back with him from Paris in the fall of that year. Feeling that some words of explanation were in order, he delivered himself of "An Answer to Future Gossip" (written late in 1928, published in January 1929), in which he refused to apologize for having bought an automobile rather than a modest bicycle: hadn't he tirelessly piled rhyme upon rhyme, 2,600 in all, to earn it? But he also suggests, rather lamely: "If there were / some danger / or // war / and mobilization, // I'll take

my steed / by the bridle / and hand it over / to comrade Commissar"
(9:392). Mayakovsky seems to have felt that his automobile, his
trips to the West, his good suits and clean shirts were a necessary
part of what he stood for: economic and cultural progress. At the
same time he continued to attack mercilessly the average Soviet
citizen's longing for a snug little place of his own (even a few bedbugs
wouldn't matter, so long as it was nice and warm), a hot samovar,
and a friendly game of cards. A poem of 1928, entitled "Idyl,"
which starts with the words, "The Revolution is over" and gives a
mock realistic description of Soviet home life, ends with these om-
inous lines:

> The Revolution is not over. / Domestic mumble
> drowns out / the rumble of approaching battle.
> Our worthy philistines / blow / their samovar pipes
> to herald the approach / of their advancing enemy. (9:342)

Mayakovsky's visit to Paris in the fall of 1928 was marked by an
infatuation more serious than the various minor affairs he had had
over the years. (Lilya Brik remained his one and only great love.)
Tatyana Yakovleva (b. 1906), a beautiful, willowy Russian emigrée,
was also bright and artistic. Mayakovsky fell in love with her and
tried to persuade her to return to the Soviet Union with him. He
also felt an urge to "squander some lines on lyrics," as he put it in
his poem "A Letter to Comrade Kostrov from Paris, on the Nature
of Love." Kostrov was the editor of *Komsomolskaya pravda* and *Molodaya gvardiya* [Young guard], who had commissioned some political poems and who must have been quite surprised upon receiving
this "Letter" from Mayakovsky. He printed it in *Molodaya gvardiya,*
though.

Soon enough, Mayakovsky had to return to the Soviet Union to
assist in the staging of his satirical play *The Bedbug* at Vsevolod
Meyerhold's theater in Moscow. Mayakovsky concentrated on correct
enunciation, leaving the other aspects of directing the play to Meyerhold. The music for it was written by Dmitry Shostakovich and
the sets were done by the popular "Kukryniksy" collective and
A. M. Rodchenko. Though it received mixed reviews, the play was
a popular success. *The Bedbug* was a rewrite of a film scenario, *Forget
about the Fireplace,* which Mayakovsky had delivered under contract
to the Leningrad film studio Sovkino early in 1928. When Sovkino

decided against using the scenario, Mayakovsky recast it as a play, retaining certain cinematic devices and effects. The play contains many motifs which also occur in Mayakovsky's occasional poetry of those years and most of which were gleaned from the pages of the daily press, *Komsomolskaya pravda* in particular.

Mayakovsky went abroad again on 14 February 1929, just after the premiere of *The Bedbug*. He went to Berlin to sign a contract for a German translation of his works, then to Prague to discuss a possible staging of *The Bedbug* (it did not work out), and on to Paris. This time his stay was more of a vacation, though it produced poetry as always, including some of his most aggressive antibourgeois pieces: his poems "An Outlandish Trick" and "La Parisienne" are reminiscent of Georg Grosz or Gottfried Benn at their fiercest. The first describes the remarkable business success of a Parisian prostitute whose main attraction is that she has only one leg. The second is devoted to a less than glamorous representative of Parisian womanhood, the lady in charge of the men's washroom at the *Grande Chaumière* restaurant. March and April found Mayakovsky on the Côte d'Azur. Having paid a visit to the gambling casino of Monte Carlo (he liked to gamble), he dutifully described it as a den of international racketeers and a cesspool of repulsive vice. When Mayakovsky returned to Moscow on 2 May, his romance with Tatyana Yakovleva was not over. He, at least, looked forward to a reunion in October, and in the meantime bombarded her with letters and telegrams.

Around this time Mayakovsky had suffered some reverses. Two of his film scenarios had been rejected by the Board of Cinematography (VUFKU). A film based on a scenario by Mayakovsky, *Dekabryukhov and Oktyabryukhov*, shown in Kiev in May and in Moscow in September 1928, had received some scathing reviews and was soon withdrawn. *New Lef*, while containing many worthwhile contributions, was not a critical or popular success. By the summer of 1928 it had become clear that the future belonged to RAPP, or rather to literary journalism controlled by the party or the Komsomol, a situation RAPP promoted. Mayakovsky had decided to leave the sinking ship and in August 1928 had handed over the editorship of *New Lef* to Sergey Tretyakov, who produced its last five issues.

In September 1928 Mayakovsky gave two public lectures under the title "To the Left of *Lef*," in which he explained the reason for his decision to leave *Lef*. Years earlier he had likened the futurists to the three hundred Spartans bravely stemming the Persian invasion at Thermopylae. Now, he said, some of the *Lef* people were still entrenched in their mountain gorges, along with other literary sects, while the Persians had long since departed. Mayakovsky pointed out that in any case he and his more progressive colleagues of *Lef* were routinely writing for newspapers and journals of mass circulation such as *Komsomolskaya pravda* and *Molodaya gvardiya,* and that all literature should proceed in this direction, eliminating narrow "sectarian" tendencies.

Upon his return from France Mayakovsky immediately plunged back into his normal hectic schedule of public appearances, meetings, and conferences. On 10 June he addressed a convention of the Union of Atheists. In July he wrote one of his most famous poems, "Verses about My Soviet Passport." In September 1929 Mayakovsky tried to save some face, and some leverage with Gosizdat too, by forming a new group, *Ref* (Revolutionary Front), whose first organizational meeting took place on Moscow in 14 September 1929. *Ref* was designed, not as an independent organization, but as more of a "workshop" group that would collaborate with RAPP (or whatever large scale organization of Soviet writers would emerge from the squabbles still going on at the time). Mayakovsky, who had always attacked others first, was now on the defensive. Appearing before a plenary session of the Executive Board of RAPP on 23 September, he had to point out that he did *not* consider himself, or his associates, "fellow travelers," since he had supported the Soviet regime from the beginning.

Also in September 1929, Mayakovsky was denied a passport and soon received word that Tatyana Yakovleva had married a French diplomat—in church, orange blossoms and all. *Ref* turned out to be stillborn, though its inaugural public meeting on 8 October was well attended and much talked about. Mayakovsky was in top form. He refused to renounce his futurist past, stressed his unremittent opposition to apolitical literature, and stuck to his avantgardist guns. On 23 October a meeting of its membership decided to undertake what would be its one positive achievement: an exhibition to mark the twentieth anniversary of Mayakovsky's career as a poet and artist. But the first public meeting of *Ref* was also its last. The general reaction to *Ref* was negative. As Sergey Tretyakov, whom Mayakovsky had abandoned to form *Ref,* put it: "We live in a period of mass organizations. Associations of the *Lef-Ref* type are doomed to play the role of specialists' corporations for the chosen few and are unfit for organized activity."

Mayakovsky must have realized the sad truth himself, for at a MAPP conference held in early February 1930 he declared, during an appearance which featured a reading of his last great poem, "At the Top of My Voice," that he had applied for membership in RAPP. A day earlier, on 5 February, he had declared (in his own name only) that "he did not perceive *Ref* as an organization distinct from the organization of proletarian writers, but rather as a school for the study of the technology of writing." By this action Mayakovsky alienated his remaining friends of the *Lef* group. Nor did it help him to bridge the gap between himself and what was now quickly becoming the literary establishment. One of the leaders of RAPP, Aleksandr Fadeev, declared: "Mayakovsky is suitable material for RAPP. As for his political views, he has demonstrated his affinity with the proletariat. This does not mean, though, that Mayakovsky is being admitted with all his theoretical background. He will be admitted according to the extent to which he rids himself of that background. We shall help him in this."

## The Final Period

Mayakovsky had high hopes that his new play, *The Bathhouse*, would do at least as well as *The Bedbug*. Public readings and radio recitals of scenes from the play, especially the famous "March of Time," seemed to justify these hopes. Mayakovsky was not quite his old self. He tired more easily, complained of a sore throat, and was sometimes nervous and irritable. But right to the end his personal appearances were almost as successful as ever. Perhaps it was a mistake to have *The Bathhouse: A Drama in Six Acts, with Circus and Fireworks* performed in Leningrad by a pupil of Meyerhold's before it saw the limelight at the master's own theater in Moscow. In any case, the Leningrad first night on 30 January 1930 was an unmitigated disaster. There were no laughs, and no applause after the first two acts. The reviews were appallingly negative. The new generation of Soviet critics, headed by that pedantic ignoramus, Vladimir Ermilov, and a good part of the audience too, simply lacked the capacity for suspension of disbelief needed to appreciate Mayakovsky's vitriolic satire on Soviet bureaucracy, combined with a Wellsian time machine and an express train into the future which throws off or runs over assorted bureaucrats, toadies, embezzlers, scribblers, a foreign capitalist named Mr. Pont Kitsch, and other objects of Mayakovsky's scorn.

The day after the Leningrad debacle Mayakovsky read "At the Top of My Voice" at the opening of his exhibition, "Twenty Years of Work," at the Writers Club in Moscow. It featured biographical material (mainly dealing with his revolutionary activities in 1908–9), photographs, material from Mayakovsky's creative laboratory (manuscripts, notebooks, drafts), books (including futurist almanacs and manifestoes), Mayakovsky's early works featuring illustrations and cover designs by modernist artists such as Larionov, Malevich, and Lisitsky, newspapers and journals (*Lef* and an assortment of other periodicals featuring works by Mayakovsky), theater (set and costume designs, programs, posters), film (posters of Mayakovsky's films, photographs of Mayakovsky in film roles), a selection of Mayakovsky's cartoons, posters, and commercials, and, finally, some documents of interest. The exhibition was well enough attended during its three weeks in Moscow. On 5 March it was transferred to Leningrad, where Mayakovsky made four public appearances in as many days. Both in Moscow and in Leningrad, Mayakovsky could not help noticing that most of his new colleagues from MAPP and LAPP stayed away.

*The Bathhouse* opened at Meyerhold's theater in Moscow on 16 March. The stage and the theater were decorated with posters bearing slogans meant to drive home the message of the play, such as: "Don't soil the theatre with slobbering psychologism! / Theater, serve communist propaganda!" One of the posters created a scandal: "You can't / wash away at once / the whole swarm of bureaucrats. / / There just aren't enough / bathhouses / or soap. // And besides, / bureaucrats get help from the pen / of critics / like Ermilov" (11:350). Ermilov, a member of RAPP, protested and RAPP pressured Meyerhold to remove the poster. Mayakovsky grudgingly agreed to have it taken down. In his suicide note of a month later, he said he regretted having done so.

The Moscow reviews were no better than those in Leningrad, though opening night was not as calamitous as it had been in Leningrad. Mayakovsky seemed gloomy on opening night, but bounced back in his usual fashion, and in several public discussions made a spirited defense of his play. He was also working on a new play, *Moscow on Fire (1905): A Mass Spectacle with Songs and Words,* one commissioned for the twenty-fifth anniversary of the Revolution of 1905. Its first performance, with 500 participants, took place at the Moscow Circus on 21 April 1930, a week after Mayakovsky's death.

*Moscow on Fire* is perhaps Mayakovsky's most avant-garde dramatic piece, a surrealist phantasmagoria. Plot is entirely abandoned. Stylized scenes from the Revolution of 1905, with no pretense whatsoever to historical veracity, antireligious and anticzarist satire, proclamations of the October Revolution shouted by a team of barkers, slogans of the Five-Year Plan and the collectivization of agriculture follow one another in rapid fire sequence. There is shooting and fireworks; bombs explode; clowns crack antireligious and anticzarist jokes. There is a lot of to-do about a critical shortage of trousers in the imperial household: his majesty is so frightened he needs a change of trousers every minute. Circus acts entertain the audience while delivering a propaganda message: for example, a giant worker (on stilts) dwarfs the police and factory owners. A huge film screen is used to make the spectacle more graphic. Premiers Ramsay MacDonald and André Tardieu, Marshal Pilsudski of Poland, and the pope appear to save a Russian *kulak,* who is being pushed underground by a mass of workers. After the pope delivers a jingle in support of *"kulaks* and religion," he and his allies are routed by an exploding bomb which scatters Soviet proclamations about. The spectacle ends with a rousing march of the workers, triumphantly carrying the class enemy's trousers on long sticks, as "Capital / —his majesty— // is forced / to change pants / more often" (11:405). Mayakovsky actively participated in the preparation and rehearsals for the spectacle.

Mayakovsky's busy calendar for March and April 1930 entirely resembles his earlier schedule. He read antireligious verses on the radio, attended meetings and participated in discussions, and kept his business appointments. On 4 April he bought a share in a housing cooperative. On 11 April he failed to make a personal appearance at Moscow University, excusing himself by illness. But 12–13 April recorded business as usual, and 14–15 April were days on which Mayakovsky had scheduled personal appearances. At 10:15 A.M. on 14 April Mayakovsky shot himself in his Moscow office. The last person to see him alive that morning was his latest flame, a young actress named Veronika Polonskaya. He left a suicide note, dated 12 April and addressed to "Everybody":

> Don't blame anybody for my death and please don't gossip. The deceased hated gossip.
> Mama, sisters, and comrades, forgive me—this is no way (I don't recommend it to others), but I have no other choice.
> Lilya, love me.
> Comrade government, my family are Lilya Brik, mama, my sisters, and Veronika Vitoldovna Polonskaya.
> If you can arrange for them a decent living, thanks.
> The verses which I have started give to the Briks, they will figure them out.
> As they say,
>   "the incident is closed."
> The love boat
>   wrecked by daily life.
> I'm all even with life
>   and nothing would be gained by listing
> mutual hurts,
>   troubles,
>     and insults.
> Good luck.
>   Vladimir Mayakovsky

> Comrades of VAPP, don't think I'm a coward. Seriously, it could not be helped. Greetings. Tell Ermilov that it is too bad I took down that slogan, ought to have fought it out. V. M.
> In my desk drawer there are 2,000 roubles, pay my income tax with it. You'll get the balance from Gosizdat. V. M.

Mayakovsky's body lay in state for three days at the hall of the Writers Federation as 150,000 mourners passed by. The body was cremated on 17 April.

The suicide note requires a few comments. The four lines of verse in it are part of a short poem found among Mayakovsky's posthumous papers, itself apparently a part of a longer "Prologue to a *Poema*," private counterpart, as it were, to the public *At the Top of My Voice*. In the original, the phrase "the incident is closed" contains a pun: *isperchen,* "over-peppered," in lieu of *ischerpan,* "closed." These lines were written some considerable time before 14 April.

The Briks, who were abroad at the time of Mayakovsky's suicide, became executors of Mayakovsky's posthumous papers. Miss Polonskaya could give no explanation for her lover's suicide. Ermilov prospered for many years as a critic, faithfully following the zigzags of the party line.

Much has been written about Mayakovsky's suicide. His own observations regarding the various speculations about Esenin's suicide apply to him as well. Anyone who has read the suicide note is in almost as good a position to make a guess as the scholars who have gathered every available piece of information on Mayakovsky's last days, weeks, and months.

The suicide motif appears early and often in Mayakovsky's poetry. According to Lilya Brik, Mayakovsky's poetic suicide threats reflected real moods of deep depresssion. There is little else to suggest that he suffered from a manic-depressive disorder.

# Chapter Two

# Poetry of the Prerevolutionary Period

## On Futurism and Symbolism

From today's vantage point, it is difficult to imagine the ambiance of the Russian avant-garde around 1912: a dynamic pluralist society in which widely diverging political, moral, and aesthetic views were professed, to be sure not without government interference, but still with a freedom unthinkable in the Soviet Union even in the 1920s. Industry, commerce, and education were developing in a capitalist society. St. Petersburg and Moscow were remarkably cosmopolitan modern metropolises: in reviewing the names of leading writers, artists, and directors of the time one finds as many non-Russian as Russian names. Russians traveled abroad freely, and many were educated at Western universities, art schools, and conservatories.

Russia actively participated in all the newest modes of thought, fashions, and fads of Western civilization. Whatever appeared in the West flourished in Russia as well: theosophy, religious revivalism, Esperanto, vegetarianism, Marxism and other revolutionary doctrines, unabashed aestheticism and hedonism, pederasty, boisterous bohemian *épatage.* Russian intellectual circles shared with the West a sense of *fin de siècle,* of impending doom.

When Russian futurism burst onto the scene it had to coexist with a number of other schools, some of them also "modernist," some not. These included old-fashioned "critical realism," Gorky's "revolutionary romanticism," naturalism, Chekhovian impressionism, symbolism of course, divided into a "decadent" and a "mystic" branch, acmeism. In the visual arts and in music too, several different schools competed for the favor of an often enthusiastically partisan public.

In poetry, the futurists competed mainly with the symbolists and acmeists. Most of the former were older (Aleksandr Blok and Andrey Bely, the most active among the symbolists, were both born in 1880, David Burlyuk, the oldest of the futurists, in 1882), while the latter were their contemporaries (Nikolay Gumilev was born in 1886, Anna Akhmatova in 1889, Osip Mandelshtam in 1891). Futurists and acmeists both challenged the positions of symbolism and had a good deal of social contact, as both groups frequented "The Stray Dog," a St. Petersburg literary café. The symbolists, by 1912 established poets and writers at the height of their careers, greeted their challengers on the whole with friendly encouragement even in the face of grave provocation.

At a gathering in honor of the major symbolist poet Konstantin Balmont (1867–1942), held on 7 May 1913, Mayakovsky said, among other things:

As you get acquainted with Russian life, you will run head-on into our naked hatred. There was a time when your searchings, your smooth, even verses, which are like the swaying of a rocking chair or Turkish divan, were close to us. You sang of a Russia of dying estates of the gentry and of naked, barren fields. We, the young, poets of the future, do not sing of these things. Our lyre rings with the present. We are a part of life. You walked up swaying, screeching stairways to ancient towers and looked down from them into an enamel distance. But now the upper floors of these towers house the offices of sewing machine companies and your enamel distances are the staging area of automobile rallies.

In the futurist manifesto "A Slap in the Face of Public Taste" (1913), the symbolists Fedor Sologub, Mikhail Kuzmin, Balmont, and Bryusov were included among those to be "thrown overboard off the ship of contemporary life." Valery Bryusov (1873–1924) came in for especially harsh criticism: "Could there be anyone cowardly enough to be afraid to strip the paper armor from the black tail coat of the warrior Bryusov?" Bryusov's critical reaction to the works of the futurists, and Mayakovsky's in particular, displayed no desire on his part to retaliate. The same is generally true of Mayakovsky's relationship with other symbolists, and acmeists as well.

There existed real and fundamental differences between symbolism and futurism, and where the mystic branch of symbolism was concerned, these differences were unbridgeable. To symbolists like

Bely or Vyacheslav Ivanov, symbolism was a world view, not merely a school of poetry. They were god seekers, passionately involved in metaphysics and religion, whereas the futurists showed little interest in metaphysics. The symbolists were highly literate intellectuals, oriented toward world literature in a historical perspective, who sustained a dialogue with the art and literature of the past. Futurism's stance was one of antihistorical urbanism or outright primitivism; it treated the culture of the past strictly as raw material, that is ahistorically. The symbolists were obsessed with a premonition of Russia's impending relapse into barbarism, which they expressed metaphorically as a new Mongol invasion. Bryusov had stated this theme in a poem of 1905 entitled "Invasion of the Huns." Mayakovsky, in one of his early poems ("There!" 1914), accepted this challenge by calling himself a "rude Hun." And the futurists generally tried to live up to that description.

The symbolists, by and large, adhered to the organic aesthetics dominant in Russia ever since the critic Vissarion Belinsky (1811–48) transplanted it into Russian literature from the German idealist philosophy of Schelling and Hegel. Its basic principle was that all art is an organic function of human life, and hence a living expression of man's national, social, and—first and foremost—metaphysical strivings. The mystic wing of symbolism also saw art as a vehicle of religious experience, related to prayer and mystic vision. Its decadent wing developed the high regard for art held by organic aesthetics to a *non plus ultra,* asserting that art is the ultimate and only purpose of human life. Futurism rejected the organic principle to embrace a formalist aesthetics. The material of which the work of art is made—the phonemes and morphemes of human speech, in the case of poetry—rather than a subject extraneous to it—an emotion, an image, a story—is seen as the artist's point of departure. Art is then the skillful manipulation of that material, and the work of art a product of that skill, rather than a mimetic representation of objective reality, or an avenue to some deeper reality.

The philosophic stance of the futurists was that of an aggressive humanism; their pattern was Dostoevsky's "man-god." At the crossroads between an ascent to God (spiritual man under God), a return to a golden age of innocent sensuality, and a straightforward development of rational humanity (where the efficient machine becomes the model of a new man), Russian futurism as a group vacillated between the second and third paths. Mayakovsky appears to have chosen the third from the beginning.

The idea that man, on his way to a higher humanity, must pass through a stage of supreme, yet machinelike, efficiency and purely mechanical mastery of nature, was not new. It had been popular in the romantic period. But while romantics and symbolists had viewed the trend toward a mechanized humanity with resignation at best, the Russian futurists greeted it with enthusiasm. One of the more striking traits of Russian futurism was its feud with the sun as a symbol of the world of the past, of nature not yet controlled by man. Aleksey Kruchonykh's spectacle "Victory over the Sun" (1913), which treats the capture of the sun by the *budetlyane* ("futurists"), was a milestone in the history of Russian modernism, and the motif of a feud with the sun occurs often in Mayakovsky. In a poem by Boris Pasternak, "picking quarrels with the sun" is seen as a part of the poet's progress ("So They Start," 1921).[1]

Symbolism had been oriented primarily toward music, considering it the one art form which could transcend the human condition. In poetic practice, some of the symbolists—for example Blok and Kuzmin—were important innovators of Russian versification, moving from traditional syllabotonic verse into various forms of tonic (accentual) and even free verse. Yet they also cultivated such traditional forms as the sonnet, and their best known poems were written in conventional meters, mostly iambic, and were remarkable more for their mellifluousness than their vigor. The futurists were drawn more to the visual arts than to music. Their tendency to break down their material—language—into its constituent elements and to reconstitute it in entirely new patterns was stimulated by cubist painting rather than by modern atonal music. Futurism's technical innovations were conceived in terms of analogous developments in modern painting. While the symbolists had tried to deal with poetic texture in musical terms, the futurists described the sounds of their verses in terms of "surface texture" (*faktura,* a term applied to the texture of canvas) and "displacement" (*sdvig,* a term which initially referred to the deformation or distortion of lines in a cubist painting).

In spite of such differences, futurism also had links with earlier Russian poetry and the other poetic schools of its day. When the futurists shouted that they were "throwing overboard from the ship of the present Pushkin, Dostoevsky, Tolstoy, etc. etc.," this did not mean that they were ignoring them. Rather it meant—particularly in Mayakovsky's case—that Pushkin, Dostoevsky, et al. were to be used for the futurist poet's own purposes—through parody, quoting out of context, shifted emphasis, and a variety of other devices. The maximum effect of these echoes from Pushkin, Lermontov, Dostoevsky, Blok, and many others is achieved only when the reader is familiar with the original text referred to. Korney Chukovsky, a perceptive critic, recalls that the young Mayakovsky used to study symbolists such as Bryusov or Innokenty Annensky "mockingly but very carefully." Mayakovsky's vitriolic putdowns of his contemporaries were based on a competent, if unsympathetic, reading of their works.

Symbolism is important for an understanding of futurism not only as a foil. The formal searchings of futurist theoreticians continued theoretical work done by the symbolists Bryusov and Bely, both of whom were creative scholars as well as poets. Mayakovsky's extensive advances in rhythm and rhyme followed a trail blazed by the symbolists. Even the futurist slogan "the word an end in itself" (*samovitoe slovo*) could be found, with a different emphasis, in Bryusov's famous lines: "Perhaps everything in life is only a means / to create brightly singing verses." The decadents' aestheticism bore the mark of resignation, while the futurists saw their principle as the beginning of great things to come.

There were connections with mystic symbolism also. The cosmic quality of futurism, a significant trait of Mayakovsky's poetry, may be seen as a vigorous and, one might say, "realized" or "materialized" version of the mystic pantheism and panpsychism of a Vyacheslav Ivanov. An important element of futurism was its penchant for popular entertainment and "happenings," spectacle and even circus. Interestingly enough, it was Ivanov, the most intellectual of the symbolists, who energetically advocated a return to the "choral tradition" and a transformation of the modern theater into a spectacle with active audience participation.

## Futurism and Painting

Widely divergent and sometimes contradictory tendencies within Russian futurism can be explained, at least in part, by the fact that it was influenced by widely divergent modernist schools of painting and sculpture. The primitivism of Mikhail Larionov (1881–1964) and others who painted pictures in the manner of a child or of a sign painter had many equivalents in futurist poetry. Mayakovsky's poem "To Signs" (1913)—a versified description of a medley of signs (fish market, "Maggi," funeral parlor, etc.)—is revealing of his general technique.

Some of Mayakovsky's early poems are patterned directly after cubist paintings. In the first lines of "From Street to Street" (1913), the verbal material is arranged symmetrically on the basis of sound, rather than meaning: "U- / litsa. / Litsa / u / dogov / godov / rez- / che. / Che- / rez, . . ." ("Street. Faces of dogs of years sharper. Through"). The poem then launches into a cityscape deformed after the fashion of a cubist painting: "iron horses / from windows of running houses / jumped the first cubes. / Swans of belltower necks, / bend in nets of wiring!" An ingenious technique of defamiliarizing the familiar is used in describing a moving streetcar as "a magician / pulling / a pair of tracks / from a streetcar's jaws," or a street corner at night: "A bald lantern / voluptuously takes off / a street's / black stocking."

One of the futurists, Benedikt Livshits, later commented that in this type of futurist poetry "the word, having gotten all too close to painting, ceased having sound." The nonobjective painting of Vasily Kandinsky, Larionov and Goncharova's rayonism (a dynamic form of space penetration consisting of rays of light), and Kazimir Malevich's suprematism (purely geometric and architectonic forms in painting) likewise had parallels in futurist poetry. The so-called "trans-sense" poetry (*zaumnaya poeziya*) of Kruchonykh, Khlebnikov, Kamensky, and others, which aimed at direct expression through spontaneous articulation or automatic writing, eschewing grammar and lexical meaning, must be seen in this context. Mayakovsky did not himself cultivate these radical forms of futurist poetry, but they influenced his poetic style.

Some aspects of Russian futurism, and of Mayakovsky's early poetry in particular, coincide with certain tendencies found mainly in German expressionism: bold outlines, screaming colors, sudden transitions, and, above all, a violent hatred of the pretty and of the sentimental, and hence a frequent search for the "unaesthetic." Mayakovsky's poetry, much as his satirical cartoons, reminds one of the German expressionists Georg Grosz and Otto Dix. Their savagely distorted cityscapes and stereotypes of modern life (the capitalist, the militarist, the priest, and other hated mainstays of the old order) are born of an anger which was also Mayakovsky's. The key device of such distortion was to deprive the hated enemy of all humanity, often by providing him with machinelike parts or extensions. It has been observed that this device is linked with an invasion of these drawings by verbal elements, such as "realized metaphor" (for example, Mayakovsky would draw his capitalists enormously fat, thus realizing the metaphoric epithet "fat capitalist"). Mayakovsky's early poetry functions through mutual enhancement of the verbal and the visual: a striking verbal image is realized visually, then expressed in precise language: "I am alone, like the last eye / of a man on his way to the blind!" ("A Few Words about Myself," 1913 [1:49]).

All his life Mayakovsky enjoyed parodying the poetry of others, especially those whom he wanted to belittle. Before the Revolution, Mayakovsky had one rival on the poetic stage, the ego-futurist Igor Severyanin (1887–1941), who had developed a personal style characterized by a slightly ludicrous penchant for decadent elegance, a touch of Nietzsche, synesthetic effects, a modern (and foreign) vocabulary, and word play. Severyanin briefly participated in the 1913 tour of the cubo-futurists before going his own way. Mayakovsky, though, continued to recite Severyanin's immensely popular poems, such as his "Champagne Polonaise," mockingly imitating Severyanin's monotonous, chanting style of recitation.

## The Futurists and Marinetti

Mayakovsky never admitted that he had been influenced by anybody in particular. He shared this attitude with the other futurists who, for one thing, always vigorously denied having been influenced at all by the Italian futurist Filippo Tommaso Marinetti (1876–1944), though Marinetti insisted that Russian futurism derived from his ideas. Mayakovsky, however, did make a bow to Marinetti at least as early as 1916 in *War and the World:* "In every youth, the gunpowder of Marinetti, / in every elder, the wisdom of Hugo" (1:240).

Marinetti's first Futurist manifesto of 20 February 1909 had appeared in a St. Petersburg newspaper on 8 March. Only on 19 November 1911 did Severyanin proclaim himself the founder of a new movement in Russian poetry, ego-futurism, and it was 1912 by the time Velimir Khlebnikov's group appeared, which called itself the "literary company of futurists" (they were generally called cubo-futurists, though, on account of their links with cubist painting). The group's manifestoes of 1912 and 1913 gave no credit to Marinetti or Franco-Italian futurism.

In 1913, by which time Russian futurism was in full swing, a good deal of information about Marinetti reached the Russian public. M. A. Osorgin's *Ocherki sovremennoy Italii* [Sketches of contemporary Italy, 1913] included the full text of Marinetti's manifesto, and may have been the main source of Vadim Shershenevich's book *Futurism without a Mask* (1913), with one chapter devoted to Marinetti. In the winter of 1914 Marinetti visited Moscow and St. Petersburg to deliver several well received lectures in French. His three Moscow lectures were not attended by any of the Russian futurists except for Vadim Shershenevich, a marginal figure. The avant-garde painters Larionov and Goncharova attended the third lecture, and Larionov engaged in a heated debate with Marinetti afterward. At the first of Marinetti's two lectures in St. Petersburg, Khlebnikov and Livshits distributed a pamphlet warning the Russian public against "falling at Marinetti's feet, thus betraying the first step of Russian art on its road to freedom and honor, and bending Asia's noble neck under the yoke of Europe." After Marinetti's second lecture in St. Petersburg (4 February 1914), a group of futurists, including Mayakovsky, published a declaration in a Moscow newspaper to the effect that they had nothing in common with Italian futurism save the name.

It is obvious that Russian futurism had much in common with Marinetti's, and that the Russian futurists owed more to him than they cared to admit: Marinetti's urbanism, his enthusiasm for modern technology, speed, and movement in general. There was also his uncompromising hatred of the old in every aspect of life, and his aggressive nationalism. But then the Russian futurists found Marinetti much too "bourgeois." They shared neither his militarism nor his misogynism. In the formal aspect of futurist poetry, one discerns a certain indebtedness to Marinetti's "wireless imagination," which passes instantanously from the past into the present or future, and from any point in the universe to any other. Farfetched metaphors, verbal acrobatics, and fractured syntax, all of which Marinetti advocated, are also prominent in the poetic arsenal of Russian futurism.

Marinetti initially denied that there was any distinction between poetry and prose, and pursued free rhythms. Rhyme, since it is followed by a pause which creates rhythm, was a suitable substitute for meter. Mayakovsky's early poetry, as soon as it emancipated itself from conventional meters, became essentially "free verse," with rhyme responsible for most of its rhythm. Marinetti eventually abandoned free verse, feeling that it pushed the poet toward purely formal effects and away from content, and Mayakovsky, too, returned to more regular rhythms after his futurist period.

Virtually all of the traits found so massively in Marinetti existed elsewhere as well. Livshits, who knew French symbolism well, relates how he read Rimbaud to David Burlyuk, who immediately transformed his impressions into verse of his own. The idea of "the sound as such," the poetization of the grotesque and the ugly, and the mixing of poetic language and vulgarisms are traits common to Russian futurism and Rimbaud, whom Mayakovsky surely knew in translation. In one major poem of his ("Verlaine and Cézanne," 1925) Verlaine appears in person. Émile Verhaeren contributed to Mayakovsky's urbanism and to his cult of energy, work, and modern life, perhaps to some extent also to his vigorously hyperbolic style. We know Mayakovsky was familiar with Verhaeren from a sympathetic and knowledgeable reference to him in an essay of 1913.[2] He also reacted with pain to Verhaeren's untimely death, in a poem entitled "Darkness" (1916). Mayakovsky's only reference to Guillaume Apollinaire, another French poet whose style resembled his own, is deprecatory ("Paris," 1923). The naive religious poetry of Francis Jammes caught Mayakovsky's attention. His "Prayer for a Star" is taken up in Mayakovsky's "Listen, If They Light Stars," a bold poetic reversal of the argument for the existence of God from design; and the French poet's "Prayer that the Child Won't Die" is parodied in the line "I like to see how children die," in "A Few Words about Myself" (both 1913).

Walt Whitman was much admired by the European avant-garde, and Mayakovsky shared this admiration. When he describes the splendor of American capitalism, he sees "a hall full of / all kinds of Lincolns, Whitmans, Edisons" (*150,000,000,* 1919–20 [2:135]), and there are some striking similarities between Whitman's poetic style and Mayakovsky's. In particular, Mayakovsky's device of making Vladimir Mayakovsky—"handsome, twenty-two years old"— the persona of his poetry recalls Whitman's "Song of Myself," begun by him "now thirty-seven years old in perfect health." There are other similarities: hyperbolic diction, paradoxic imagery, frequent personification and metamorphosis, free verse (which has always been a rarity in Russia). There are important differences also. Mayakovsky's vision is more mannered, metaphoric, and artful. He is virtuosic where Whitman seems deliberate, and lacks Whitman's disarming naiveté and boundless zest for life.

In Mayakovsky's early poetry the poet's persona is often identified with a martyr of the church, or with Jesus Christ Himself, always in travesty. Very likely this derives from the pervasive Nietzscheanism of Russian symbolism and the Nietzschean archetype of the suffering god, popularized in Russia by Vyacheslav Ivanov. I. Kostovsky has drawn attention to the striking similarity of Mayakovsky's apostrophe to God the tormentor in *The Backbone-Flute* (lines 69–101) and the sorcerer's lament—addressed to "that cruellest hunter, God the unknown,"—in part four of *Thus Spake Zarathustra.*[3]

## Organized Futurism

In view of the many different sources of, and influences on, Russian futurism, perhaps a well-defined futurist movement existed only in the minds of outsiders lacking exact knowledge of the theory and practice of individual futurists. It is important to note that the futurists of 1912 and 1913 were apolitical: the fact that Mayakovsky had a revolutionary political past was accidental.

Khlebnikov's first decidedly "futurist" piece, "Temptation of a Sinner," appeared in October 1908, before Marinetti's *First Futurist Manifesto* (1909). Later (in *A Slap in the Face of Public Taste*) Burlyuk falsely claimed that the first *Hatchery of Judges,* containing several clearly "futurist" pieces, had also appeared in 1908. It actually came out in 1910, two months before Nikolay Kulbin's almanac *Studio of Impressionists,* which contained two of Khlebnikov's most famous futurist poems, "Incantation by Laughter" and "Thickets were Filled with Sounds." Among the contributors to *Hatchery of Judges, I* were most of the would-be futurists of the Hylaea group, with the notable exception of Livshits and Mayakovsky.

The group to which Mayakovsky belonged late in 1912 called itself Hylaea *(Gileya),* after the Greek name of the area on the Black Sea where the Burlyuks lived. Livshits, who coined the name, associated it with the savage freedom of the Scythian horsemen who had lived there in the days of Herodotus. Scythianism, in obvious conflict with the urbanism of Marinetti, accorded with the mood not only of certain leaders of the Russian avant-garde in painting, such as Goncharova and Larionov, who were interested in folk art, but also with that of the futurist poets Khlebnikov and Kruchonykh, and their linguistic theories. Mayakovsky shared these tendencies only to a limited extent, but for the time being he was a Hylaean. He was one of four who signed the manifesto of the Russian futurists which appeared in a pamphlet, *A Slap in the Face of Public Taste* (1912). The others were David Burlyuk, Aleksey Kruchonykh, and Viktor Khlebnikov.

The manifesto, while decisively rejecting "the Academy and Pushkin, more incomprehensible than hieroglyphics" and all contemporary literature ("the perfumed fornication of Balmont," "the dirty slime of books written by innumerable Leonid Andreevs"), had only a short positive program. And that amounted to a demand for unrestricted use of neologisms and a radical retooling of the existing literary idiom, in the name of the "New Approaching Beauty of the Word-in-Itself." The term *samovitoe slovo,* "word-in-itself," coined by Khlebnikov, was the real *pièce de résistance* of the manifesto.

*A Slap in the Face of Public Taste* contained several interesting poems and prose pieces, among them the first two published poems by Mayakovsky, both unremarkable. From here on the Hylaea group, small though it was, became and remained very active for several years. The year 1913 was marked by group appearances throughout the country, by the staging of Kruchonykh-Matyushin's *Victory over the Sun* and Mayakovsky's *Vladimir Mayakovsky: A Tragedy* in St. Petersburg, and by the publication of the miscellanies *A Hatchery of Judges, II, The Croaked Moon* (the title page identified the contributors as "futurists" of "Hylaea"), Khlebnikov and Kruchonykh's *The Word as Such* (with a cover drawing by Kazimir Malevich), and of a number of pieces in verse and in prose in various other collections and periodicals. In all of these enterprises Mayakovsky was clearly the star, and David Burlyuk the capable impresario.

The Hylaeans immediately found themselves in competition with several other groups which also called themselves futurists and put out their own pamphlets and almanacs. There were the ego-futurists in St. Petersburg; the *Mezzanine of Poetry* group in Moscow, headed by Shershenevich and the painter Lev Zak, among whose publications was the "Crematorium of Common Sense" (1913); and the

Centrifuge group, also in Moscow, whose first and only miscellany, *Lyrics* (1913), had contributions by Boris Pasternak (1890–1960) and Nikolay Aseev (1889–1963).

In 1914 a number of further futurist collections appeared, still under such outlandish titles as *Milk of Mares* and *Roaring Parnassus*, still full of outrageous attacks on Russian literature in general; still illustrated by modernist artists who would one day be famous (Ivan Pougny, Pavel Filonov, Olga Rozanova, Alexandra Exter, the Burlyuks); still full of typographic quirks borrowed from Marinetti. The poetry in these publications was often interesting and sometimes remarkably good.

In March 1914 the first and last issue of the *First Journal of Russian Futurists* appeared in Moscow. It was also the first (and last) attempt to end the internecine struggle of competing factions within the Russian avant-garde and to unite all futurists under the same cover. The outbreak of the war marked the beginning of the end of futurism as organized group activity, as the public understandably lost interest in futurist extravaganzas. On the other hand, the futurists discovered that they had become a part of the literary establishment and could publish in established periodicals. They were admitted to the famous "Stray Dog" literary café in St. Petersburg, and by the winter of 1915 Mayakovsky was the main attraction there. But the "Stray Dog" was closed by the police in March of that year, and the various futurists continued their careers on their own, some as writers and poets, some as painters. Only after the Revolution of 1917 did several of the Hylaeans meet again to resume organized activity.

## The Doctrines of Futurism

Russian futurism was moved by conflicting tendencies. On the one hand it strove for modernity, urbanism, technology, and a mechanical and formalist conception of art; but, on the other, it tended toward atavism, primitivism, surrealist and automatic creation. With this conflict on their hands, the futurists could agree on one thing: their hatred of existing bourgeois culture, including of course its literature and art. When the futurists spoke of slaps in the face of public taste, they were quite serious. David Burlyuk's lines (in *The Croaked Moon*):

The sky is but a corpse, no more!

The stars are worms, drunk with mist.
The stars are worms, a purulent, live rash.

were typical for the movement. Mayakovsky forever retained a hearty dislike for the conventionally beautiful or sublime.

The futurists' hatred of the past often emerged in a pointed antihistoricism and anachronism, also a trait which Mayakovsky retained to the end. The futurist aesthetics emphasized the difference between art and nature, an emphasis which served the urbanist wing of futurism well. Mayakovsky was fascinated by electric street lamps more than by the moon. He welcomed the hectic rhythms and jagged contours of the modern metropolis. One aspect of futurism's anti-naturalism is its tendency to conceive the world in terms of things and material relationships ("reification"), reversing the animism of romantics and symbolists. In the early Mayakovsky, human characters are often reduced to cardboard figures, signs, or objects.

The futurists, by and large, were formalists who saw a poem, or a picture, not as a "reflection" or "expression" of anything, but as a "thing" made by a skilled craftsman. They liberated art from its ideological and moral moorings, reducing it to technique. They were ready to jettison everything that had preceded them and to start from scratch, from "the word as such," or even from "the sound as such." Benedikt Livshits put it this way: "The only way a poet can be possessed by matter is to be possessed by the material of his art, to become immersed in the element of the word." David Burlyuk declared, in a lecture of 1912, that the identity of an entity created by a painter should be entirely irrelevant to the viewer, who should be concerned only with the manner in which an object was reproduced on a surface. The futurists also stressed the artificial nature of their poetic creations by emphasizing typographic detail, including graphic metaphors. Kamensky printed a poem describing his flight over Warsaw in pyramid at the tip of which was a single letter. The reader was instructed to read from bottom to top, to get the impression of an airplane vanishing in the distance. In his poem "An Automobile Ride" (1913), Mayakovsky interspersed his description with shreds of signs whirling by: "post," and a full line later, "office." Burlyuk and others used different shapes and sizes of letters and signs to enhance the impression created by a poem.

Nevertheless, for Mayakovsky the aural aspect of poetry dominated its visual aspect. His habit of printing his verse "like steps of a stair" rather than in straight lines served to signal pauses. Many of Mayakovsky's early poems were printed in normal stanzaic form, though. The futurists also claimed that they "had ceased to look for meters in text books, because every new movement gives birth to a new free rhythm" *(A Hatchery of Judges, II)*. Mayakovsky maintained that he never knew the difference between an iamb and a trochee, but he could write perfect iambic and trochaic (as well as dactylic, amphibrachic, and other) lines. He simply adjusted meter to his rhythms, moving up and down the scale from syllabotonic to free verse.

The cornerstone of futurist poetics on the level of sound was what Kruchonykh called the "texture" *(faktura)* of speech sounds. In *A Hatchery of Judges, II,* the futurists declared that they understood "vowels as time and space" and "consonants as color, sound, and smell." Kruchonykh went on to classify the sound texture of speech as "tender" / "coarse," "heavy" / "light," "harsh" / "muted," "dry / moist," and even "sweet" / "bitter." Mayakovsky retained some elements of this conception, preferring sounds which he classified as coarse, heavy, and harsh, such as *r, sh,* and *shch.*

The second cornerstone of futurist poetics was *sdvig*—"displacement, dislocation, deformation"—another term borrowed from cubist painting, which emphasized deformation of structure and its deciphering. Kruchonykh and Khlebnikov put it this way: "Futurist painters like to use sections and particles of bodies, while futurist artists of the word like to use dissected words, half-words, and their quaint and clever combinations" *(The Word as Such,* 1913). Futurist theoreticians soon realized that this principle applied to every level of poetic art: sound, rhythm, syntax, imagery, and meaning. They also discovered that multiple perspective, simultaneity (showing different aspects of the same form at once), dislocation of structure, and other varieties of "impeded perception" could be employed in poetry no less than in painting. Mayakovsky's early poems show numerous instances of all there types of deformation, and consequently often resemble a rebus. A peculiar kind of displacement widely utilized by the futurists was shifting the reader's (or listener's) attention from one aspect of a verbal structure to another, such as from meaning to sound structure, or from syntax to rhythm. For example, Mayakovsky's rhymes are sometimes so obtrusive as to distract attention from the meaning of a line, and the rhythm of his free verse often goes against natural stress contours.

The third cornerstone of futurist poetics, unlike the first two, belonged to the realm of intuition and mysticism. It was *zaum'*, "the transrational" or "metanoumenal." The idea behind it was that of immediate expression through speech sounds, on the theory that certain sound structures are anchored in the depths of the subconscious and can be released by the creative act of a poet. Kruchonykh, who formulated the theory of transrational poetry, believed that these sound structures are universal and prenational. As Livshits put it, "this was a return to primeval chaos. . . . into the soft, amorphous substance of the word not yet infused with meaning." Mayakovsky did not experiment with glossolaly, dadaism, imitation of bird voices, automatic writing, and surrealism, as did Khlebnikov, Kruchonykh, Zdanevich, and others. He was always a highly conscious artist, keenly interested in technique.

The futurist conception of "the word as such" or "the word-in-itself" is more apparent in Mayakovsky's art. Khlebnikov, in particular, was preoccupied with the roots of the Russian language and their original meaning, which led him to create many neologisms, on the one hand, and to delve into the deep structure of forms and meanings ("etymologism"), on the other. Mayakovsky shared both of these tendencies. Also, he was at all times a believer in, and a user of, the power of the word as such—as a fetish, as a whip, or as a narcotic. He liked to hypostatize individual words, to make them palpable.

Much as the poetry readings of the futurists included lectures about their work, so their published poetry received a running commentary in a steady flow of manifestoes, essays, articles, reviews, and notes. Some of Mayakovsky's early lecture notes are extant, and he published some twenty articles and notes in various journals and newspapers before the Revolution, most of them on modern art and poetry. Significantly, his first two articles (1913) dealt with the cinema and appeared in *Cine-Journal,* a magazine devoted to this new art form. Mayakovsky boldly asserted that the cinema was destined to rejuvenate a stagnant theater, enslaved by its various utilitarian commitments, and return it to its proper domain of free creativity.

The young Mayakovsky's ideas were not all original and he did give credit to his sources, his fellow futurists in particular (not to Marinetti, though) as well as Parisian cubism. He strongly defended the autonomy of art. In his essay "The Painting of Today" (1914), he declared: "It was not so long ago, either, that nobody even dreamed of art as an end in itself. Doubled up under the load of the idea of dumb animal existence and the struggle for survival, we forced even the artists to join in our screams for bread and justice"(1:286). He went on to point out that art could be subjected to forms of enslavement that were even worse, such as painting "the fat hams of drunken mistresses" (1:286) (a quote from Marinetti!). Mayakovsky suggested that there were better ways to attain the mimetic, didactic, and moral purposes of art, and that art ought to be left alone to pursue its "only and eternal goal: free play of man's cognitive faculties"(1:288). The young Mayakovsky went so far in his defense of the autonomy of art as to claim that, "while, as a Russian, I hold sacred our soldier's every effort to tear away an inch of soil from the enemy, I must also think [as an artist] that the whole war was thought up for the sole purpose of allowing someone to write one good poem" ("A Civilian Shrapnel," 1914 [1:304].)

To Mayakovsky the futurist, art meant a new and different vision, achieved through deformation, dislocation, and deconstruction, which in poetry meant dissonant sound patterns, new word forms, syntactic inversion, shifted accents, and farfetched metaphors. One of his earliest poems articulates this program perfectly:

> At once I blotched the map of humdrum life
> by splashing some paint on it from a glass
> and, on a dish of meat-jelly, displayed
> the slanting cheekbones of the ocean.
> On the scales of a tin fish
> I read the call of new lips.
> But you,
> could you
> play a nocturne
> on the flute of a drainpipe?
> (1913; 1:40)

The young Mayakovsky fully accepted the futurist approach to art through its material: the word as an end in itself is a recurrent topic in his early essays. Mayakovsky also believed that only the futurists could draw out all the corollaries of that position: "(1) word against content, (2) word against language (literariness, academism), (3) word against rhythm (musical, conventional), (4) word against meter, (5) word against syntax, (6) word against etymology" ("He Who Came Himself," 1913 [1:365–66]). The symbolist decadents, he wrote in another essay ("Without White Flags," 1914), who also asserted that the word was an end in itself, resembled the ancient Egyptians, who knew how to stroke a dry black cat to produce electric sparks but never learned how to use electricity to run streetcars. Such decadents as Balmont kept producing poetic platitudes, while the futurists had the courage and ruthlessness to bring the word under a master innovator's conscious control.

The young Mayakovsky was a competent art critic, who enthusiastically, yet knowledgeably, embraced the modern art of his day. "We ought to have," he wrote in "The Painting of Today," "instead of paintings that are camels or other such beasts of burden, serving to convey 'the rational meaning of the subject matter,' paintings that are merry barefooted dancers, whirling in a passionate and brightly colored dance" (1:293). It has been suggested that Mayakovsky is here alluding to Matisse's panneau "The Dance." Altogether, Mayakovsky felt that modern art was like "a prophet, announcing to the world the luminous laws of a new life to come" ("A Quick Glance at the Vernissages," 1914 [1:341]).

## Mayakovsky's Prerevolutionary Futurism

Mayakovsky's prerevolutionary poetry bears all the marks of futurism, considered a decadent bourgeois school by postrevolutionary Soviet critics. It contains much *épatage,* gratuitously provocative language and imagery, and just *Bohème.* There is also a great deal of formal experimentation: the futurist canon of shifted construction, cubist dissection, and depiction, not of objects but of their constituent elements, is much in evidence. All of this together creates a strong effect of estrangement.

The main subject of Mayakovsky's futurist lyrics, to quote the title of an early poem (1913), is "The Hell of the City." Mayakovsky's cityscape is that of German expressionism. It captures the city's macabre absurdity, its fearsome ugliness, and its deadening mechanization of life. In the streets and taverns of Moscow, Mayakovsky discovers gruesomely "unaesthetic" imagery. There is, for example, the sad "Case of a Bandleader" (1915). Insulted by a nightclub owner, "dripping with ladies' flesh," the bandleader lets his trumpet slap a bearded patron's "stuffed mug with a handful of brassy tears," directs his trombones and bassoons to bowl over other patrons until the last of them, having failed to creep out the door, "dies with his cheek dipped in gravy," then makes his musicians "howl like beasts" as he himself sticks his trumpet into the corpse's teeth, blows it and listens to its wails resounding in the victim's bloated belly. Finally, "In the morning, when the owner, / so mad he hadn't even eaten, brought him his termination notice, / the bandleader had long since turned blue on the chandelier, / swinging and turning bluer" (1:90).

Mayakovsky's farfetched metaphors, in the process of becoming "realized," create a fantastic new world, yet one still linked to reality, much as in cubist painting. Many of the early poems can be read as a rebus or charade. It has been pointed out, however, that Mayakovsky's metaphorically deformed descriptions are still amazingly accurate. The following poem, entitled "Seaport" (1912), may serve as a case in point:

> Bedsheets of water under her belly,
> torn into waves by a white tooth.
> Sirens wail—as though the brass of pipes
> were pouring out love and lechery.
> Lifeboats in their cradles,
> snuggling up to the teats of their iron mother.
> In the deaf ears of steamers
> there burn earrings of anchors.

The egocentric quality of Mayakovsky's poetry emerges early from the background of the "hell of the city," as Mayakovsky searches for a poetic "I." The first person singular form he uses so often is not always to be taken literally. Frequently it is a kind of cosmic "I," a realization of the "poet equals creator" metaphor, with the poet's consciousness assuming universal, or even cosmic, proportions:

> In a second
> I shall meet
> the monarch of the heavens—
> and I shall simply kill the sun!
> ("I and Napoleon," 1915)

More commonly, though, the poet's persona appears hopelessly es-tranged from the world as Mayakovsky devises ever new metaphors to express his alienation. He likens himself to an ostrich shorn of its feathers to become one with Russia, that cold and fierce country ("To Russia," 1916). He feels alienated even by virtue of his own size: "If I were / little, / like the Great Ocean, / I'd rise to my tiptoes on its waves / and I'd be the tide fondling the moon. / Where could I find myself a beloved, / such as myself?" ("To Himself, Beloved by Him, the Author Dedicates these Lines," 1916).

Altogether, the young Mayakovsky's moods are not as optimistic as true futurist moods should have been. Rather they exhibit pain, revulsion, and despair. It is no wonder, then, that the persistently recurring themes of self-apotheosis and suffering conjoin to engender an identification with Christ and suffering figures of world literature in his poetry. In his poem "To All" (1916), that identification with suffering is extended to the suffering of animals: a white bull with his neck festering under the yoke and flies swarming over his sores, or a moose with his antlers caught in some wiring, his bloodshot eyes bulging.

All the moods and motifs of Mayakovsky's futurist period are recapitulated in *Vladimir Mayakovsky: A Tragedy* (1913), actually a lyric monologue with some personalized props, such as "an old man with dry black cats, several thousand years old," "a man without one leg and one eye," "a man without a head," and such. It is likely that N. N. Evreinov's *Theory of Monodrama* (1908) had some influence on Mayakovsky. It is significant that the play was staged at the same theater, on alternate days, as Kruchonykh's demonstratively futurist *Victory over the Sun,* with which it shares such motifs as hostility to the sun: "We shall pin the suns on our lasses' dresses, / we shall forge silvery broaches from the stars" (1:157). It also advertises the universal language of *zaum':* "And you will / grow lips // for immense kisses / and a language / native to all nations" (1:154). Furthermore, the key device of both plays is "realized metaphor," which creates an estranged world where things turn into subjects and abstract concepts into things: *"Old man with cats:* There you see it! Things must be chopped up! It's not for nothing that I've recognized an enemy in them!—*Man with a stretched out face:* But maybe things must be loved? Maybe things have a different soul?" (1:158).

This device also works as a means of trivializing metaphysics: "I was looking for / her, / my unseen soul, / so that between my wounded lips / I might put healing flowers. *(Stops.)* And again, /

like a slave / in bloody sweat, / I rock my body in madness. / However, / I did find her once, / my soul. / She came out / in a light blue robe, / and said: / 'Sit down! / I've waited for you a long time. Won't you have a glass of tea?' " (1:159). This whole passage is based on a pun: *dusha,* "soul," is used as a word of endearment ("my dear," "darling").

The real poetry in *Vladimir Mayakovsky* comes from Vladimir Mayakovsky's lyric effusions. As Viktor Shklovsky puts it: "The poet has spread himself out on stage, holding himself in hand as a card player holds his cards. Here's Mayakovsky the deuce, the three, the jack, the king. The game is staked on love. The game is lost."[4] The theme of the poet's self-immolation is stated in the very prologue: "How could you understand, / why I, / calmly, / through a thunderstorm of ridicule, / carry my soul on a dish / to the dinner of future years" (1:153). Vladimir Mayakovsky's monologues are a mixture of confession, emotional outpourings, *épatage,* and flight of surrealist imagination, all propelled by puns and realized metaphors.

While *Vladimir Mayakovsky* was a novelty, the young Mayakovsky's verse epics *(poema)* were closer to a tradition stemming from the Byronic verse epic. Mayakovsky's *poema* moves even further away from plot and toward expression of personal experience, and away from picturesque description to a chaotic panorama of the poetic persona's consciousness. It is constructed as an inner monologue, whose changes of scenery, subject matter, and mood follow quite unpredictable associative thought patterns, which are often dreamlike.

The persona revealed in these monologues is by and large simply Mayakovsky's. Indeed, he often identifies himself either by name or by introducing members of his family, friends, or a personal experience. That experience encompasses the whole range of a modern intellectual's interests, including literature, the arts, science, and contemporary events, major as well as trivial. Mayakovsky's language base is the colloquial idiom of an educated Russian. Whenever poetic, ecclesiastic, legal, or other special terms show up, as they do often, they appear in quotation marks, as it were, and are invariably "reaccented," which creates an effect of travesty.

## The Early Epics

*A Cloud in Trousers: A Tetraptych* (1914–15) is the best known of Mayakovsky's verse epics, at least in the West, although it is inferior

in nearly every respect to certain later pieces. The best thing about
it is its title, explained in the prologue:

> If you want me to,
> I'll be mad with flesh
> —but, like the sky, changing its hue—
> if you want me to,
> I'll be irreproachably tender,
> not a man, but a cloud in trousers! (1:175)

After the Revolution, Mayakovsky related that the poem was initially called *The Thirteenth Apostle,* and was conceived as a revolutionary epic: each of its parts proclaimed a challenge to the old
order: "Down with your love!"—"Down with your art!"—"Down
with your social order!"—"Down with your religion!" There is little
support for this *ex post facto* interpretation in the text itself, although
motifs of blasphemy, rebellion, and violence occur intermittently
throughout the poem. The cosmos, God and the whole arsenal of
religious symbolism, the history of mankind, in short everything
that is or might be, provides Mayakovsky with metaphors to express
the love and suffering of Vladimir Mayakovsky. Also, as Dostoevsky
once observed sarcastically, the great works of world art and literature find their ultimate purpose in serving as material for the puns
and witticisms of "the Russian genius":

> What do I care abour Faust,
> by the magic of rockets
> gliding with Mephistopheles along the parquet of the skies?
> I know:
> a nail in my shoe
> is more nightmarish than a Goethean fantasy!
> (1:183)

The ostensible cause of Vladimir Mayakovsky's anguish is a young
lady named Mariya, who makes a few brief appearances ("You entered, / abrupt, like 'take it!' / torturing the suede of your gloves, /
and said: / 'You know, / I'm getting married' " [1:178]), and the
poem contains passages where emotion is credibly expressed, as, for
example, in this magnificent dance of Mayakovsky's nerves when
he realizes that he is being stood up by his ladylove: "I listen, /
quietly, / like a sick man from his bed, / a nerve leaps down. / And

there, / he takes a few steps first, / just barely, / then starts running, / excited, / distinct. / Now he and two more / dash about in a frenzied tap dance. // The ceiling plaster comes crashing down to the floor below. // Nerves— / large, small, many!— / leap about madly, / but now their legs are giving way!" (1:177–78).

But the whole thrust of this, as of Mayakovsky's other verse epics, is toward a cosmic Golgotha, combining images of titanic hubris and blasphemy with images of crucifixion and martyrdom. Mayakovsky—who will "use the sun for a monocle," who will "lead Napoleon on a leash, like a pug dog," before whom "all earth will spread herself out like a woman, her flesh fidgeting, wanting to give herself to him"—also fancies himself "a spat-at man of Golgotha." He continues: "But to me, / my people, / even those of you who abused me, / you are dearest and nearest to me. // Have you seen / how a dog licks the hand that beats it? // I, / laughed-at by the tribe of today, / like a long / scabrous anecdote, / I see him who will come over the mountains of time, / whom no one else can see" (1:184–85). Thus, with all his blaspheming, Mayakovsky becomes a genuine, thirteenth apostle:

> And while my voice
> shouts bawdy words,
> hour after hour,
> all day long,
> maybe, Jesus Christ is sniffing
> the forget-me-nots of my soul.
>                                        (1:190)

Mayakovsky's imagery in *A Cloud in Trousers* is interesting throughout, though frequently a bit labored. But his declamatory verse (rhymed free verse all the way) is fresh and vigorous. His rhymes are consistently ingenious, and there is a great deal of play with inner rhyme, assonance, and alliteration.

*The Backbone Flute* (1915) is a somewhat shorter, tighter, and even more intense version of *A Cloud in Trousers*. The title is explained in the prologue: "Today I shall play the flute / on my own backbone" (1:199). The object of the poet's love is now a very real Lilya (though she is not named in the text) instead of some shadowy Mariya, and Mayakovsky's feelings are believably those of Catullus for his Lesbia—"I hate and love!":

> I trample miles of streets with the sweep of my step.
> Where can I go with such hell concealed within me!
> What heavenly Hoffmann
> dreamed you up, accursed one?!
>
> (1:200)

The metaphor of the demonic *femme fatale* is promptly realized as Mayakovsky declares that if one made the sign of the cross over his beloved's marital bed, "there surely would be a smell of burnt wool, / and a devil's flesh would go up in sulfurous smoke." Mayakovsky then quickly shifts to his favored cosmic imagery as he begs God, "the Almighty Inquisitor," "to tie him to comets, as to horses' tails, and whirl him through space, rending him against the jags of stars" (1:200), or better, "string him up, the criminal, using the Milky Way for a gallows," all this and more, but "take away the accursed one, whom He made his beloved" (1:201–2).

The next two major epic poems—*War and the World* (1915–16) and *Man* (1916–17)—appeared in print only after the Revolution, but they belong to the domain of futurist poetics. Some critics have argued that, since the grotesque nightmares of futurism had become reality in the holocaust of the World War, Mayakovsky's *War and the World* was in fact a truthful reflection of that monstrous reality. If this is so, it is hardly an objective reflection of the reality of war. Once again Mayakovsky's point of view is egocentric: a world ablaze becomes an extension of the poet's persona. Mayakovsky identifies with victim and tormentor alike. It is he who "stands on the place of execution, gasping for his last breath of air" (1:230). But it is also "I, / Mayakovsky, / who carried / a beheaded babe / to the idol's altar." It is "I, / Mayakovsky, / Vladimir, / who with drunken eyes enveloped the circus" (1:231), when the lions gave out a roar. It is "I, / Mayakovsky, / who in the vaults of Seville, twisted the joints of heretics / on the rack" (1:232). When Mayakovsky exclaims; "People! / Dear people! / For Christ's sake, / for the sake of Christ, / forgive me!" he clearly alludes to the principle of shared universal guilt proclaimed by Father Zosima in *The Brothers Karamazov*.

Though *War and the World* has been likened to Picasso's "Guernica," its poetic horrors inevitably fall short of the real horrors of war. But its first part—a Breughelian vision of the decadent Babel that was prewar Europe—has great power. The outbreak of the war, in part 2, is viewed through the eyes of a satirical cartoonist: "Heidelberg students, / galloping astride their Kant! / Knives clenched in their teeth! / Sabres bared!" (1:219). France, Russia's ally, and Russia herself are given similar lines, and by no means more complimentary ones. Part 3—in which the events of the war up to the end of 1915 are recognizable—ends with this *danse macabre:*

> And when all those killed
> had fallen silent,
> and batallion upon batallion
> lay there,
> death came running
> and danced over the corpses,
> noseless Taglioni of the skeletons' ballet.
>
> (1:228)

Mayakovsky's self-identification with victims and perpetrators of horrors in part 4 (quoted earlier) forms a transition to the theme of resurrection and a new life in part 5: "Let me bleed to death, hacked to pieces, / but with my blood I shall eat away / the name of 'murderer,' / with which man is branded" (1:230). Part 5 brings a resurrection of those killed in the war, as severed legs come looking for their bodies and torn off heads call out the names of their owners. There follows a universal festival of love and brotherhood, for a new and heroic race of men will arise:

> Men will be born,
> real men,
> more compassionate and better than God Himself.
>
> (1:233)

*Man* was written in 1916 and the first half of 1917, before the October Revolution, and it appeared in print in February 1918. It shows Mayakovsky at the height of his creative powers as a lyric poet. *Man* is a polyphonic composition with a plot (though of a very special kind), several leitmotivs modulated and set off against one another in a lyrical "minor" and a satirical "major" key, challenging ambiguities, and some hauntingly emotion-laden passages. Rhythmically, too, *Man* is more varied and more appealing than the earlier verse epics. The prologue contains three leitmotivs stated in a liturgic prose recitative:

The hand of the sun, minister of the world's sacraments, absolvent of all sins, rests upon my head.

The vestment of Night, the most devout of the religious, is wrapped around my shoulders.

I kiss the Gospel of a thousand scrolls in which the days of my love are recorded.

(1:245)

In the text of the poem what may be called rhymed prose—like that of a Russian folk tale—alternates with regular iambic passages of a singularly driving rhythm. The *boutade* and satire are all in the former, the poetry almost all in the latter form. The brief epilogue is again a liturgic recitative, ending with the Orthodox equivalent of "May he rest in peace!"

The plot structure derives from a parody of an Orthodox saint's life, whose sections are entitled: "The Nativity of Mayakovsky"— "The Life of Mayakovsky"—"The Passion of Mayakovsky"—"The Ascension of Mayakovsky"—"Mayakovsky in Heaven"—"The Return of Mayakovsky"—"Mayakovsky to the Aeons." The whole poem is saturated with quotations from, and free variations on, biblical and liturgic texts (Noah, the Star of Bethlehem, Cana of Galilee, Golgotha, the Apocalypse, etc.), always travestied.

The "nativity" section is a wry self-parody of earlier egotistic verse: "whoever kissed me / will say / if there could be / any juice sweeter than my spittle." The "life" section is, as Lawrence L. Stahlberger has pointed out, a set of variations on a theme from Aleksandr Blok's "Danse macabre":[5]

> Night, street, lantern, drugstore,
> Senseless, dim light.
> Live yet another quarter of a century
> And all will be the same. There's no escape.
> You'll die. So you'll take it from the start
> And all will repeat itself as before:
> Night, the icy ripples of the canal,
> Drugstore, street, and lantern.

Night, street, lantern, and drugstore all appear in Mayakovsky's text as the poet who "would have liked to bathe everybody in his love" finds himself a prisoner, with "the globe of the Earth / chained to his feet," or even worse, "locked / forever / into a senseless tale" (1:251). From such metaphysical (Nietzschean or Dostoevskian) dread of entrapment in a cycle of "eternal recurrence," Mayakovsky drifts into even more tormenting anguish at the sight of "Him, the Sovereign of All, / my rival, / my invincible adversary" (1:252). "He"— never identified—is he who "ordered the late Phidias / to make him some buxom broads / from marble" (1:253), he whose "nimble cook, / God, / created pheasant meat for him / from clay," he who has "legions of Galileos / scurrying about the stars through the eyes of telescopes" (1:254) to find him the most priceless of females. Soviet critics have identified "Him" with capitalism, but this will not do. Rather, "He" is that in humanity which denies man's divinity, freedom, and creativity, that which Dostoevsky called "the spirit of Nonbeing and destruction," that side of man which insists that everyday existence *(byt)* is life.

The "passion" of Mayakovsky begins as "the townspeople go / to bathe in His plenitude" (1:254) (a parodic "dig" at Nietzsche). "She," the poet's beloved, is among them. Mayakovsky cannot stop her and must watch as she bends over His little finger, where three bristel like hairs grow below a diamond ring. Her lips whisper something to those three hairs, "calling one 'my little flute,' / the second 'my little cloud,' / and the third by the unspeakable radiance / of some name / which I had just only created" (1:255).

Mayakovsky's "ascension" is dominated by the suicide motif: a bullet, a razor, and poison at a drugstore counter. But in the end Mayakovsky unexpectedly overcomes the laws of physics and levitates himself around the drugstore counter, through the ceiling, and up into the sky.

Mayakovsky "in heaven" offers some comic relief. Life in heaven is hopelessly boring. "The central station of all phenomena / with a mess of plugs, levers, and handles" offers little interest. "The smithy of time" which forges "the terrible landslide of years" (1:261) offers little to cheer about.

Upon his "return," Mayakovsky finds the earth changed somewhat by tunnels, superhighways, and multitudes of airplanes, but still run by that same "baldheaded / invisible one, / that chief dancing-master of earthly cancan, / once in the form of an idea, / once somewhat like a devil, / once shining like God, concealed by a cloud" (1:266).

In the last section, "Mayakovsky to the Aeons," the poet returns to his old apartment on Zhukovsky Street to learn that "It has been Mayakovsky Street for a thousand years: / here he shot himself at the door of his beloved" (1:269). He walks up the stairs, driven by an urge both to see his beloved and finally to get even with "Him." But in what used to be his bedroom he discovers a certain Nikolaev, a civil engineer, and his wife, "a strange woman, / stark naked, / the corners of her mouth trembling" (1:271). The poem attains a magnificent finale with two iambic quatrains:

> All will perish. All will come to naught.
> Even he who is the mover of life
> will burn out the last ray of the last suns
> over planets cast into darkness.
> And only my pain is sharper,
> as I stand engulfed by fire
> on the everburning pyre
> of an unthinkable love.
> (1:272)

The brief epilogue is a dirge for a vast but lonely soul expelled into an alien universe.

In *Man*, Mayakovsky employed many of his familiar futurist devices and images, yet moved away from futurism into an unmistakably romantic poetic world: the world of Jean Paul's "Oration of a Dead Christ, given from the Edifice of the Universe, on how there is no God" (1796–97), Byron, Lermontov, Heine, Hugo, and Nietzsche. It is a world of metaphysical anguish and painful alienation. The persona of the poem is Christ, martyr, dandy, or clown, depending upon the context, but all these personae are characteristic of romantic poetry. Also, Mayakovsky's cosmic imagery develops into the familiar "inner sky," "night of the soul," "inner sun," "abysses of the soul," and other romantic conceits. However, few romantic poets could equal Mayakovsky in inventiveness, intensity, and vigor in presenting these images and moods.

*Man* is also among the most euphonically orchestrated of Mayakovsky's poems. Its first line may serve as an example: "zvenyáshchey ból'yu lyubóv' zamolyá" (atoning for love by ringing pain, 1:245). It contains no fewer than five different pairs of sound repetition: zvenyashchey—zamolya (this alliteration of the first and last word

serves as a clasp); *b*ol'yu lyu*b*ov'; *bol'y*u—za*mol*ya; bo*l'yu*—*lyu*bov';
and the chiasm *bol'yu*—*lyubov'*, where the second word ("love") is
a mirror image of the first ("pain").

# Chapter Three

# Poetry of the Revolutionary Period

## The Avant-Garde and the Revolution

Mayakovsky had known the horrors of war by hearsay, but he saw the collapse of civilized urban life during the years of revolution and civil war with his own eyes. The grotesque, the absurd, and the unspeakable became a part of everyday life. Some poets were awakened by these horrors to write strong lines of compassion, pain, and outrage, the symbolist Maksimilian Voloshin, in particular. Mayakovsky also wrote some poems reflecting genuine civic and human concern. For example, "Two Not Quite Ordinary Occurrences" (1921), written at a time when famine on the Volga was depopulating entire villages, takes hunger as its subject. Among assorted other vignettes—including even a case of cannibalism—the poet draws the image of an old man whom he once saw stealing away with the head of a dead horse, then describes a crowd of people eating smelly salt herring with their hands at what had once been an elegant café. The poem's call for an all-out war on famine has a ring of earnest sincerity, even though it is couched in the usual style of the propaganda slogans of the day.

However, on the whole Mayakovsky's poetry of the revolution and civil war years is rarely serious in an immediate, artless way. That was because Mayakovsky and his fellow futurists had decided that they could join the Bolshevik Revolution while remaining avant-garde artists. In 1918–19 all left-wing artists—suprematists, cubists, constructivists, and others—were called "futurists." They all hoped that the Soviet regime would create for them conditions under which they could realize their innovative ideas: popular theater of grandiose proportions, monumental abstractionist sculptures, streets and squares gaily decorated with their paintings, mass poetry readings: in general they wanted to see their art penetrate the broad masses of the people. To some extent these ideas were realized: poets and musicians did go into the factories to perform before audiences of workers, artists did hang their paintings in the streets, paint railroad cars, and draw propaganda posters. There were a few mass spectacles with audience participation.

The two revolutions of 1917 brought the Moscow cubo-futurists Burlyuk, Kamensky, and Mayakovsky together again as a group. Between the fall of that year and April 1918 they gave frequent poetry readings at their own café of poets. On 15 March 1918 the first and only issue of the *Futurist Gazette,* a one-sheet newspaper, appeared. It contained two manifestoes, "Decree No 1 on the Democratization of the Arts" and "Manifesto of the Mobile Federation of Futurists," signed by all three poets, and an "Open Letter to the Workers" signed by Mayakovsky, who also contributed two poems: "Revolution: A Poetic Chronicle" and "Our March." In his "Open Letter" Mayakovsky deplored the fact that the old art of assorted *Aidas* and *Traviatas,* with various Spaniards and counts, was still in vogue, even though the victorious working class deserved better. "Only an explosion of the Revolution of the Spirit will cleanse us of the trash of old art," he exclaims. The revolution of content, he suggests, is unthinkable without a revolution of form, which latter he summarily equates with "futurism." Mayakovsky, who always remained loyal to futurism as a movement and to his fellow cubo-futurists, sincerely believed that Futurism was indeed the very vanguard of progress. His poem of 1918, "Order to the Army of the Arts," ends with the rousing summons: "Into the streets, futurists, / drummers and poets!" (2:15). In a poem of 1919, "With Comradely Greetings, Mayakovsky," the futurists are likened to the three hundred Spartans who stemmed the Persian tide at Thermopylae.

In their manifesto the futurists had demanded "separation of art from the government" and a transfer of all facilities to the artists themselves. But they soon realized that they could do even better: they could make the program of the avant-garde the cultural doctrine of communist society. This seemed feasible because few prerevolutionary artists of any stature would cooperate with the new regime. As early as the winter of 1918 Osip Brik had founded a literary society called "Art of the Young" (IMO), whose main function was the publication of works by its futurist and formalist members. IMO put out a futurist miscellany, *Ryebread Word,* and a collection of formalist essays, *Poetics,* as well as four pieces by Mayakovsky. Among IMO's members were the cubo-futurists Mayakovsky, Burlyuk, Kamensky, Khlebnikov, and Kruchonykh, and also Nikolay Aseev and Boris Pasternak, as well as the formalist critics and theoreticians Boris Kushner, Boris Eichenbaum, Viktor Shklovsky, and Roman Jakobson.

In the summer of 1918 Brik and Mayakovsky, along with the entire IMO group, were asked to join the Department of Fine Arts (IZO) of the Peoples Commissariat of Public Education, headed by A. V. Lunacharsky. This meant a subsidy from the Commissariat to IMO's publishing ventures, and a chance to propagate futurism through the Commissariat's weekly *Art of the Commune.* Mayakovsky joined IZO in the fall of 1918; and published most of his poems of 1918–19—primarily versified editorials—in *Art of the Commune.* Among the weekly's other contributors were the artists Malevich, Chagall, Kandinsky, and Pougny, and the critics Boris Kushner, Shklovsky, and Brik.

In the winter of 1919 Brik and Kushner attempted to create a futurist cell even within the Communist party. When a Collective of Communist Futurists *(Komfut)* was established in St. Petersburg, Mayakovsky was not an officer of that organization, because he was not a party member (Brik and Kushner were). *Komfut* issued a manifesto and held some meetings, but the venture did not succeed, for the party never gave it any official sanction. In May 1919 the publishing branch of the Commissariat of Public Education was taken over by the State Publishing House *(Gosizdat)* and henceforth Mayakovsky had to deal with that agency, which had little enthusiasm for futurism. A Communist party decree dealing with the Proletarian Culture *(Proletkult)* movement and dated 1 December 1920, made it clear that the Soviet authorities not only did not encourage futurism, but actually considered it harmful.

Two main factors contributed to the downfall of futurism. The first was the aesthetic conservatism of the Soviet leadership. The official policy of the government was to preserve the cultural legacy of feudal and bourgeois Russia for the enlightenment and enjoyment of the working masses. Gorky took charge of a publishing project designed to make the classics of world literature accessible to millions of readers. When Mayakovsky suggested that the classics "had escaped into their *Collected Works,* as into ratholes, but to no avail, even if Gorky himself was spreading the wings of his worn authority

over them like a hen over her chicks" (*150,000,000* [2:159]), he
met with little sympathy from the Soviet leadership. In vain did
Mayakovsky explain that "throwing the classics overboard" meant
eliminating their influence on contemporary art and literature, not
their physical destruction. He did not realize that Soviet art and
literature would tend precisely to return to nineteenth-century
models.

The other factor that worked against futurism emerged during
the extended and acrimonious debate between the futurists and the
*Proletkult*. Although the *Proletkult* likewise eventually failed to gain
the approval of the Party, in 1920 it had as many as 80,000 members
working in its studios and workshops and organized in 300 local
groups, and was bringing out some twenty periodicals. The poets
and artists of the *Proletkult* sought to express their proletarian mentality, their feelings of triumph, and their hopes for a bright future.
Being aesthetically unsophisticated, they naturally utilized the form
of what few examples of art or literature they were familiar with,
and so the form of their works tended to be that of bourgeois art
and literature at their worst. The futurists, therefore, wanted to go
beyond a "proletarian mentality" to a wholly new, modern mentality
in a totally new, modern environment of functional objects designed
by modern artists and verbal stimuli that would enhance man's
analytic capacities and modernize his consciousness.

The *Proletkult* wanted no part of all this. One of their spokesmen
wrote: "Before its death, bourgeois art developed various hideous
lumps and malignant growths, one of which is futurism." It was
precisely the charge of "bourgeois decadence" that Mayakovsky never
successfully refuted. Actually, Mayakovsky's ideology was impecca-
ble. If he was guilty of any deviations from the party line, they
were invariably to the left. Mayakovsky's cartoons and propaganda
verses always presented the capitalist West, with which the Soviet
government was soon enough seeking to establish normal diplomatic
relations and much needed trade, as an ugly bourgeois with a huge
belly and a giant cigar in his mouth. Similarly, the Soviet regime's
internal enemies—*kulaks*, priests, NEP-men, and so on—were always cast as hideous monsters, wholly deprived of a human identity.
Even in those early years he combated the inertia of daily living
(*byt*), which slowed down the drive toward a communist society,
with uncompromising vehemence:

More terrible than Wrangel[1] is the daily routine of the philistine.
Quick,
wring your canary's neck,
lest communism
be killed by canaries!

("About Trash," 1920 [2:75])

Behind these unrelenting attacks there stands a distinct positive program. In "The Fourth Internationale" (1922), after denouncing the various manifestations of philistinism for some 200 lines, Mayakovsky exclaims:

Making heads start by its explosions of thought,
booming away with its artillery of the heart,
there rises from the depth of time
a different revolution,
the third revolution
of the spirit.

(2:103)

He sees himself as a torchbearer of that "third revolution," who "points / his finger—his line of verse— / into the future, / and grows into the future / with the eye of his imagery" (2:100).

In his "Fifth Internationale" (1922), Mayakovsky clarifies what he means by all this: "I want to join the ranks / of Edisons, / the ranks of Lenins, / the ranks of Einsteins" (2:108). However, there is an ambiguity inherent in Mayakovsky's future-oriented humanism. On the one hand, his man of the future (Lenin is his chief example) is more thoroughly human than the various types of *Übermensch* found in literature, who tend toward "godmanhood" or "mangodhood." But on the other hand, Mayakovsky's "humanity" often resembles a collection of efficient machines: "Who will ever / accuse us of idleness? / We grind the brain with the file of language. / Who is superior: the poet / or the technician / who / leads people toward material welfare? / Both are. / Hearts are no different from motors. / The soul is exactly like a cleverly constructed machine. / We are equals" ("The Poet-Worker," 1918 [2:19]).

Mayakovsky always wished to assure his public that the poet was an eminently useful member of the new society, so he was eager to show that poetry, no less than engineering or science, was concerned with real things. In a poem of 1922, "I Love," he repeats the challenge of "But You, Could You?" of 1913: "You know French. / You do division. / Multiplication. / You decline a noun famously. / All right, decline it then! // But tell me, / could you sing a duo with a house? / Do you understand the language of streetcars?" (4:87).

So there is, on the one hand, Mayakovsky the materialist. But he also displays—particularly in his poetry of the revolution and civil war years—a strong liking for metaphysical and cosmic imagery. Even the poets of the *Proletkult* saw the Revolution as an event of cosmic significance, and used a great deal of cosmic imagery in their revolutionary poetry. That was exactly the way Mayakovsky saw it, too:

> Line up with those beaver collars,
> Generals Constellations,
> Line up with the coveralls,
> millions of the Milky Way
> (*150,000,000* [2:149])

In *150,000,000,* even Martians join the fray, as "the very globe of the Earth / splits up into two halves" (2:149).

Assertions such as "the course of the planets, / the survival of great powers / are subject to our will" (this one in "Revolution: A Poetic Chronicle," 1917 [1:139]) irritated the communist leadership, because they put the party's realistic political goals on the same level as cosmic fantasies. Nor was Mayakovsky's "cosmism" the only unrealistic trait of his art: his liking for the forms of popular entertainment, circus, and showmanship generally led him away from the "content" of art and toward pure form. Needless to say, all these "antirealist" tendencies were a carry-over from prerevolutionary futurism. Indeed, in his "Order to the Army of the Arts" (1918) Mayakovsky advertised the notion that "the letters *r, sh,* and *shch* were good letters" (2:14), more suitable, apparently, for promoting the Revolution than other letters of the Russian alphabet. Such ideas derived from the aesthetics of the "sound as such."

## The Revolution and Revolutionary Poetry

As Mayakovsky developed into a Soviet poet, the scope of his poetry expanded. To begin with, he wrote a series of programmatic poems on the role of the poet in a revolutionary and post-revolutionary society, including "Order to the Army of the Arts," "The Poet-Worker" (both 1918), and "The Third Internationale" (1920). Here Mayakovsky consistently demanded that revolutionary poetry have an appropriately revolutionary form and tirelessly combated any return to old forms and old ideas. His exercises in a new *ars poetica* are often witty and interesting.

And then Mayakovsky paid tribute to classicism with the ode. Nobody could have imagined that Mayakovsky would begin to write genuine odes within a few years of his futurist beginnings, least of all the poet himself. Yet a piece such as "Vladimir Ilich!" (1920) is decidedly a solemn ode, down to its last rhyme:

> I would not be a poet,
> if
> I were not to sing of this—
> dotted with five-pointed stars, the sky
> of the vast firmament of the RCP.
>
> (2:34)

The last rhyme is "pel: RKP" ("sing: Russian Communist Party").

These years also saw the first of Mayakovsky's revolutionary marches, "Our March" (1917), "Left March" (1918), and others. Mayakovsky's marches retained many of the traits of his futurist poetry: sharp, syncopated rhythms, an emphasis on the isolated word and on the sound as such, and striking imagery. The following lines from "Our March" illustrate all these traits:

> The bull of days is skewbald.
> Slow the oxcart of years.
> Our god is the run.
> Our heart is a drum.
>
> (2:7)

Here the first and the third lines contain three one-syllable words each *(Dney byk peg—nash bog beg)*, while the last two ("bull skewbald"—"god run") form one of Mayakovsky's characteristic rich rhymes.

Mayakovsky's battle against Soviet philistinism through poetic satire began early: "About Trash" (1920–21) is a good instance of this. But some poems surprise us with their satire. One of Mayakovsky's most famous poems—"An Extraordinary Adventure that Happened to Vladimir Mayakovsky in the Summer, while Vacationing," written in 1920, is a ballad in iambic quatrains[2] with the same driving rhythm so characteristic of *Man* and *About That*. It describes a visit which the sun paid Vladimir Mayakovsky one summer day, at his invitation. The two chat and discover they have much in common. They make a pact to cast light, each after his own fashion, upon the grey trash of the world, dispelling "the wall of shadows, / gaol of night" (2:38) wherever they can.

Another genre which one might not have expected from Mayakovsky appears in a six-line poem entitled "Grief" (1920):

> Vainly a desperate wind
> thrashed about madly.
> Drops of blackening blood
> cool on the roof gables.
> And a widowed moon
> came out for a lonely walk in the night.
>
>                                                    (2:41)

The vast bulk of Mayakovsky's work in those years, though, was propaganda poetry. He produced hundreds of cartoons and jingles which appeared in the windows of ROSTA from 1919 to 1922, such as number 539:

I. Comrades! Why aren't there any Soviets in Europe as yet, and the bourgeois are in power? (Shows a fat capitalist sitting on top of a factory, champagne glass in hand.)

II. Because over there Menshevik-Reformists have ingratiated themselves with the workers. (Shows an elderly intellectual type holding back a worker.)

III. They will promise the workers heaven knows what, but in reality they are the true friends of the bourgeois. (Shows the Reformist embracing the fat capitalist.)

IV. Remember this, comrades: There is only one workers party—the communists! (Shows a worker with an RCP flag.) (3:214)

Not all the ROSTA pieces are this primitive, though most are. Among them are several parodies of familiar classics: Heine's "Grenadiers" become three beaten White generals; Goethe's "Flea" becomes a ballad about the king of England and his trained flea, the

White general Denikin; Marshal Piłsudski becomes the "dashing merchant" from a ballad by Ivan Nikitin, and so on.

Mayakovsky's propaganda poetry is consistently vicious, hitting below the belt and kicking an enemy already down, such as the clergy or the Mensheviks. "Soviet Alphabet" (1919) offers this couplet on the latter: "Mensheviks are such people / as will sell their own Mother" (2:93). Often enough Mayakovsky gives his imagination free rein in futurist fashion, as, for instance, when he threatens peasants who might desert from the Red Army with the return of their landlords, who will not only whip the peasant but actually make the peasant's wife suckle the landowner's pet dog ("Tale of the Deserter Who Set Himself up Quite Nicely, and About What Befell Him and the Shirker's Family," 1920 [2:61]).

Mayakovsky's skill as a political cartoonist is not quite on the level of his verbal virtuosity. Mayakovsky became a fine craftsman who could produce a desired figure with a few surehanded strokes, but his drawings lack the finesse and nuance that his verbal artistry will sometimes convey even to a crude propaganda jingle. His workers, peasants, soldiers, capitalists, priests, etc. are stereotypes without the leaven of imagination, iconic signs, not symbols. Hence they do not inspire any emotion—hatred, revulsion, contempt, solidarity, sympathy, or compassion—as the drawings of a Georg Grosz do. But Mayakovsky's drawings did successfully lay down the party line for the illiterate and semiliterate masses.

Mayakovsky quickly made himself into a master of political invective. He can be full of righteous wrath, as when he curses the Western powers for letting Russian peasants on the Volga starve to death ("Swine!" 1922). He will solemnly declare that the day of reckoning for international capitalism is near ("My Speech at the Genoa Conference," 1922). He will play fast and loose with the facts as he slanders and denounces Western statesmen, as in a "Ballad about Emile the Valiant" (1922), in which he viciously attacks Emile Vandervelde, a Belgian socialist who came to Moscow in 1922 to defend a group of Russian Socialist Revolutionaries, whose show trial marked the suppression of their party.

### Mystery-Bouffe

It is not surprising that Mayakovsky should have developed into a master of the propaganda spectacle. *Mystery-Bouffe* is what its title suggests: a morality play *(mystère)* in travesty. Like all topical art, it was subject to change depending upon political developments. It exists in two versions, of 1918 and 1921. The "Prologue" of the latter version contains the argument of the play: "The gist of act one is this: / The Earth has sprung a leak. / There is a stampede. / Everybody is on the run before the flood of the Revolution. / Seven clean couples / and seven dirty couples, / that is, / fourteen pauper-proletarians / and fourteen bourgeois-gentlefolk, / and among them / with his pair of tear-stained cheeks / a little Menshevik. / The North Pole is all awash. / The last refuge is about to go under. / So all start building / an ark / a very big ark, in fact. / In act two / folks are en route in their ark: / Here you have your monarchy / and your democratic republic. / At last, / overboard, / the Menshevik's wails notwithstanding, / the clean ones are flung head first. / In act three it is shown / that workers / don't have to be afraid of anything, / not even the devils in hell. / In act four— / laugh louder!— / the halls of paradise are shown. / In act five, economic ruin, / opening its huge mouth, / destroys and devours things. / Though we had to work on an empty belly, / we still / defeated economic ruin. / In act six / you have the commune, / so everybody / sing along at the top of your voice! / Look out, then!" (2:248–49).

*Mystery-Bouffe* resembles a medieval morality play in that it is set on earth, in hell, and in heaven, and also in that it is stylistically polarized: there is an element of utopian and cosmic allegory, delivered in mannered "high style," and there is an element of homespun folk satire, delivered in rhymed lines of uneven length (the *raeshnik* of Russian folk poetry). The latter prevails. As a travesty on various biblical themes (the Flood, the New Jerusalem, Heaven and Hell), *Mystery-Bouffe* features a great deal of antireligious propaganda. When Christ approaches the ark, walking across the sea, one of the "dirty ones" observes that "so far the Almighty has always turned his backside to us, / now he's trying to trap us with Christ," and another shouts: "We don't need him! We won't let the rascal come close! The mouths of the hungry are not for prayers" (2:210). Whereupon Christ changes into a man of the thirtieth or fortieth century, who promises them paradise—but on earth, not in heaven.

With God dead, and hell exposed as not nearly so terrible as the hell-on-earth of war and exploitation, Nature becomes man's primary enemy: "Down with Nature's outrageous yoke!" (2:300). A "dirty" machinist takes over the Lord of Sabaoth's lightnings in an allegory of Lenin's electrification program, and at the end the victory march of the "dirty ones" takes them "up solar scales, up the stairs of rainbows" (2:302) and on to a conquest of outer space.

The allegory operates on a more mundane level in songs by "machines," "things," and "foodstuffs," who chiefly apologize to the "dirty ones" for having served the "clean ones" so long, in spite of having been made and serviced by the "dirty ones." These details are reminiscent of *Vladimir Mayakovsky,* and indeed *Mystery-Bouffe* is linked to cubo-futurism in its wealth of blatant sound symbolism and cubist sound patterning, whimsical imagery, and quite irresponsible mixing of semantic levels. That mixing may be seen in the list of *dramatis personae* (of the second version), which includes allegoric figures, for example, a "man of the future"; types, such as an Indian rajah or a Russian black market operator among the "clean ones," and smith, laundress, and machinist among the "dirty ones"; political caricatures (Clemenceau, Lloyd George); "saints" (Methuselah, Jean-Jacques Rousseau, Leo Tolstoy); devils; angels; and an assortment of "things."

*Mystery-Bouffe* is a mixture of the ultramodern and of elements that derive from hoary antiquity: one critic justifiably recognized in it "the ancient but unflagging spirit of Attic comedy." *Mystery-Bouffe* was composed as a "montage of gags" and other attractions years before Eisenstein formulated his theory of film. It was also the first experiment, jointly undertaken by Mayakovsky and Meyerhold, in the "circusization" of the theater that later became Meyerhold's trademark. Yet it also contained the time-honored rhythms of the barker and the ditty, the gibing and jeering of the carnival parade.

### *150,000,000: A Poem*

*150,000,000: A Poem* (1920–21) is a synthesis of Mayakovsky's revolutionary poetry. Like *Mystery-Bouffe,* it combines utopian allegory, political satire, and futurist grotesque; it also contains many echoes of familiar mythology: the Bible, the Orthodox liturgy, Homer, Rabelais. The plot revolves about a mythic Armageddon in which the giant Ivan (= 150,000,000 cold, hungry, desperately poor Russians) ultimately vanquishes an equally mythical Woodrow Wilson, ruler of Chicago and the whole capitalist world. In flagrant disregard of Leninist doctrine, the assault on Chicago starts as an elemental tidal wave of 150,000,000 head of starving humanity, soon joined by "billions of fishes, trillions of insects, animals, wild and domesticated" (2:120), and finally by an army of "millions of defaced, broken, and ruined things," all shouting "let's go, let's go!" in unison (2:122).

The god in whom they trust is the man-god, builder and mechanic; their faith is in electricity and steam. Their march will bring them to mastery of all the wealth of the world, to tearing down the old everywhere, to breaking down the wall of time, and to painting a thousand rainbows in the sky. The departure of the 150,000,000 culminates in perhaps the most rousing piece of poetry in the Russian language, a revolutionary march whose effect is based entirely on rhythm and sound modulation. Different forms of the verbs *bit'*, "to beat," and *barabánit'*, "to drum," are combined with the noun *barabán*, "drum," and other words which help create the desired sound effect. The march begins thus:

> Mímo
> > bárov i ban'.
> Bey, barabán!
> > > Barabán, barabán'!
> Býli rabý!
> > Net rabá!
>
> By
> > bars and baths.
> Beat, drum!
> > > Drum, beat the drum!
> They were slaves!
> > > No more slaves!
> > > (2:127)

Clearly, the revolutionary "content" of this march is secondary to its cubist "form."

The scene then shifts to Chicago, a fantastic place of incredible splendor, wealth, and technological miracles, whose name lends itself to alliteration with various words in *ch*. Chicago is the home of Woodrow Wilson, likewise an utterly fantastic figure. He is enormously fat, and "His clothes are so fine, / as though there weren't any at all. / Wilson's underpants / are no underpants, but a sonnet, / yards from their *Onegin*" (2:134). In Wilson's antechamber, waiting to be of service, are soprano Adelina Patti (who died in 1919, at a ripe old age!), Walt Whitman in a tight-fitting tuxedo, Shalyapin, "ready to sing at a moment's notice," the scientist and Nobel laureate Ilya Mechnikov, whose job it is to clean candlesticks, and others, who have come to Chicago to gorge themselves on the ample foodstuffs available in Chicago markets.

This idyl is interrupted by the news of a terrible storm which soon turns out to have been caused by the advance of the mountainous giant Ivan, who has broken through the Dardanelles, passed through Rome and then Gibraltar, and is now marching on Chicago. The whole world, like some volcanic lava flow, streams to join Ivan, or to seek refuge with Wilson. The whole world is turning either red or white, as Woodrow Wilson prepares to meet Ivan in single combat. In the meantime the animal world, things, and the entire cosmos take sides. Race horses join Wilson while dray horses join Ivan; similarly limousines and trucks, decadents and futurists, and even constellations and the Milky Way. As the battle is joined, trucks pursue billionaires' wives, table legs spear capitalists, Rockefeller is garrotted by his own collar. Wilson, for his part, sends into battle economic ruin, famine, lice, and epidemics. When they too fail—the Peoples Commissariat of Public Health defeats epidemic disease and the Soviet Economic Council routs the black market—Wilson sends forth his last army, "the poisonous army of ideas: democratism, humanism, and all those other -*isms*" (2:157). Philosophers, professors, priests, and writers all take their turn trying to stop Ivan—and fail. The classics of literature vainly seek refuge in their *Collected Works,* under Gorky's protection. The futurists rout the culture of the past, "scattering its shreds in the wind, like confetti" (2:159).

And then Wilson is suddenly turned to ashes as "the squadron of the past goes down to the bottom of the sea" (2:159) and the battle is over. An epilogue features a peace festival of the future: visiting Martians, the Sahara desert transformed into a Garden of Eden, a celebration of the memory of humans, animals, and things of the past, all of which "in spite of everything did their job, in spite of everything put in some work" (2:163).

*150,000,000* is a modern poem. Its essentially visual imagination is that of an animated cartoon, and realized metaphor is its key device. Even more than *Mystery-Bouffe, 150,000,000* is a medley of moods, styles, rhythms, and levels of language. Its basic approach, though, is one of travesty, in the sense that the relation between signifier and signified (say, Mayakovsky's Woodrow Wilson and the real Woodrow Wilson, who was in the White House at the time) is arbitrarily distorted—often, though not always, to serve Mayakovsky's propaganda purposes. As Mayakovsky said—both in the poem and elsewhere—he did not care whether a capitalist politician wore whiskers or was clean shaven, it was his deeds that mattered. Aside from its questionable propaganda value, *150,000,000* was a successful *tour de force* as a fusion of futurist poetics, revolutionary enthusiasm, and Mayakovskian declamation in hundreds of entertaining and a few score great lines of poetry.

## About That

*About That* (1923), preceded by a much shorter *poema,* "I Love" (1922), also devoted to the peripeties of the poet's romance with Lilya Brik, is Mayakovsky's most interesting and masterful longer work. It belongs to the same genre as *A Cloud in Trousers, The Backbone Flute,* and *Man.* Like them, it is a medley of the ridiculous and the sublime, of genuine pathos and uproarious grotesque, of personal statement and literary parody. In spite of its length (over 1,800 lines), the poem is distinctly lyrical and emotion-laden, even hysterical at some points. In contrast to the roughshod, syncopated rhythms of Mayakovsky's political verse and the driving trochaic folk rhythm of much of his didactic poetry, *About That* is dominated by fluid iambs (familiar from *Man*) and the irresistible lilt of anapests and amphibrachs, always kept on edge by a sufficient number of irregularities.

"That" is, of course, "love." After a half-teasing, half-fervent prologue which may be read as an encomium to Love, the poem for some 1,500 lines deals with the ups and downs of Mayakovsky's love. Only toward the end does a philosophical—or social, if one prefers—angle intrude: the tribulations of love must become a thing of the past as "lovers" become "comrades." Soviet critics have, however, suggested that *About That* be read in the context of the debate over the relationship of the sexes in communist society, which ran the gamut from Aleksandra Kollontay's advocacy of "free love" to naive attempts to subject love to Communist party discipline. In fact, some critics have suggested that the basic conflict in the poem is between "the fiery wings of October" and other symbols of a communist future, of which there are some in the poem, and the "snug little burrow" of personal life. F. N. Pitskel' has described *About That* as "a poetic narrative about how the hero futilely strives to make people heed his plea for help, to make the whole world respond to his call, 'comrade!' "[3] The hero's pleas go unheeded because everybody wishes to remain in his own little sphere of life. Even his beloved follows him from a personal feeling of pity, and not because she shares his thirst for universal, all-encompassing love.

Some writers among Mayakovsky's contemporaries solved this problem by making their heroes' devotion to their class and to the party overcome even the strongest erotic attraction, family loyalty, or longing for personal happiness. Mayakovsky is not so optimistic, at least in *About That*.

*About That*, like Mayakovsky's earlier poems, introduces many details from the poet's personal life. The title of part 1—"The Ballad of Reading Gaol"—is incomprehensible to a reader who does not know that *About That* was occasioned by a lovers' tiff which caused Lilya to banish Mayakovsky from her presence for two months, confining him to his room in Lyubyansky Passage. He felt as though he were serving a prison term.

The engine of the poem's plot is once again realized metaphor. The ring of Lilya's telephone is accompanied by so much tension it causes an earthquake. The cook who lifts the receiver immediately turns into the second in a fatal duel. The telephone call effects the poet's metamorphosis into a shaggy bear, as he is overwhelmed by animal jealousy. He sheds enough tears to float away on his pillow, which becomes an ice floe as the bear turns into a polar bear. Perched on his ice floe, he reaches St. Petersburg only to encounter his own double, who for seven years has contemplated suicide on a Neva bridge and wondered if the other Mayakovsky has become a contented philistine. The suicidal double assures him he will not allow such a thing to happen.

Part 2 is entitled "The Night before Christmas," possibly after a fantastic tale of Gogol's. Mayakovsky finds himself back in Moscow, where he searches for a savior. His first encounter is with Jesus turned Young Communist, the occasion for a parodic "romance" in archromantic, Lermontovian trochaic pentameter. He then meets his family ("Auntie! Sisters! Mama!"), whom he begs to help him save the suicide back in St. Petersburg. But in vain: they are the sort who "substitute tea for love, who darn your socks in lieu of love." Mayakovsky stumbles on to yet another Christmas party, this time with some old friends, and there runs into yet another double, a domesticated, philistine version of Vladimir Mayakovsky. He seeks to arouse the compassion of his friends for the lonely suicide, but all his entreaties go for naught, even these heart-rending lines:

> Let's say, I'm a bear, to put it bluntly . . .
> But then there's verse . . .
>                         You can skin him, you know?!
> Give him a lining of rhymes—
>                         and you've got yourself a fur coat!
>                                                     (4:163)

Mayakovsky's attention now turns to Böcklin's "Isle of the Dead" (his key image of philistine banality), which launches him on a new sequence of mad dreams, until he finds himself walking up the stairs ("just as / Raskolnikov / after the murder, / when he came back to ring the bell" [4:167]) to the apartment where he knows his beloved is celebrating Christmas with her friends. He hears music, dancing, and tipsy voices, while praying that "her unbearable voice" may not be among them. There follows a long apostrophe to "her," which leaves it unclear whether she loves him. When it appears that she might save him, his suicidal St. Petersburg double of seven years ago returns to remind him of his calling. Mayakovsky now turns into his poetic persona of "Man," scapegoat of all mankind, "redeemer of all earthly love." He suddenly finds himself made a spectacle of and laughed at on Montmartre as he asks the world to unite under the red flag. He then becomes airborne and lands on the cupola of St. John's in Moscow, which is, strangely enough, also in the shadow of Mount Mashuk of the Caucasus, site of Lermontov's last duel. Mayakovsky implores an angry crowd gathered below to spare him, but is shot to pieces until only a red rag is left of him, flying over the Kremlin. But the sky continues to sparkle with lyric stars and Ursa Major (the Great She-Bear, in Russian) takes to "troubadouring"—"to make herself queen of poets" (4:177), sister of the bear who keeps bawling his verses as he flies through a starry universe.

The epilogue is a petition to the chemist of A. D. 3000 who will resurrect Mayakovsky. He advances various arguments as to why he should be deserving of such attention and concludes the tirade with a flourish of solemn verses to Faith, Hope, and Love. *She* was beautiful, so they will resurrect her too, most probably, and the two of them will be reunited in a world of universal love where the world is Father and the earth Mother.

*About That* has more of a plot, surrealist though it may be, than any of Mayakovsky's earlier verse epics. Nevertheless, it is basically a montage of conceits, some of which might be called "gags," with a good deal of satirical grotesque. In the following lines Mayakovsky recognizes the daily habitat of his own double, "a boarder in knickerbockers":

> From mattresses,
>                           raising the rags of bedding,
> bedbugs waved their little legs, greeting me.
> The whole samovar sparkled, spreading its rays about,
> as though it wanted to embrace me with its handles.
> Dotted by flies,
>                           wreaths of flowers
>                                on the wallpaper
> crown my head all by themselves.
> All rosy in the gloss of their icons,
> bugler-angels play me a flourish.
> Jesus,
>           lifting his
>                crown of thorns,
> greets me politely.
> Marx,
>           sporting a bright red frame,
> faithfully serves the philistine's fancy.
>                                (4:161–62)

Other conceits are less prosaic. Many lean toward the melodramatic. Here the poem's persona meets his suicidal double:

> Seven years I've stood here,
>                           gazing into the waters,
> Tied to the railing by the ropes of my lines.
> For seven years these waters haven't taken their eyes off me.
> When,
>           when will the hour of deliverance strike?
>                                (4:151)

The familiar images of loneliness, alienation, and martyrdom of the poet appear in a variety of artful conceits. Mayakovsky identifies with Pushkin and Lermontov, great poets killed in senseless duels, victims of society, and also with Christ. The poet's death, transfiguration, and resurrection are familiar motifs. Incidentally, the theme of resurrection by scientific methods was widely discussed in Russia after the work of Nikolay Fedorov (1828–1903), a mystic philosopher.

*About That* hardly qualified as a contribution to the "building of socialism" in the Soviet Union. In fact, *Lef* tried to fit it into its own program by introducing it as an exercise in metric polyphony— which it was, among other things. Rhythm is used symbolically: for example, the excited, syncopated rhythm of the two-step at the drunken Christmas party is interrupted by the flowing iambs of the poet's lyric outcry. The poem also features a great deal of cubist play with sound patterns, apparently for no other purpose than to show off the poet's virtuosity.

Mayakovsky, in his own comments on the poem, stressed its social content: "The crucial thing in the poem is everyday life *(byt)*. And by this I mean a way of life which has not changed at all and which is our greatest enemy, turning us into philistines" (4:436). Later on, in 1928, in line with the aesthetics of *New Lef,* Mayakovsky began to interpret his love poem in the light of "literature of fact." Neither viewpoint is wrong, nor is the standard Soviet interpretation which regards the tragedy of love in *About That* as an expression of the frustrations of the NEP period, caused by a clash of the old and the new value systems. But the work's greatest value lies in its poetry, the product of a marvellously fertile imagination on every level of verbal creativity.

## Chapter Four

# Poetry of the Postrevolutionary Period, Plays, and Work in Other Art Forms

## The Trials of *Lef* and *New Lef*

*Lef* (1923–25) was the organ of a coalition of futurists (specifically, the Moscow Association of Futurists [MAF]), formalists (specifically, the Society for the Study of Poetic Language [OPOYAZ]), Vsevolod Meyerhold's State Theatrical Institute (GITIS), the Art Council of the Moscow *Proletkult,* the Institute of Artistic Culture (INKHUK, of which Kandinsky and Brik had been chairmen in 1922), and the Higher Artistic-Technical Workshops (VKHUTEMAS), created as a replacement for the Academy of Fine Arts, closed in 1918. It was through Brik's efforts that the constructivists of INKHUK, such as Aleksandr Rodchenko, Varvara Stepanova, and Lyubov Popova, became contributors to *Lef* as graphic artists. *Lef* was planned as an international organ, and the first issue carried translations from foreign literatures (including excerpts from *Babbitt* by Sinclair Lewis). Regular foreign contributions were planned, but failed to materialize.

As a publishing firm, *Lef* did not exist very long. As early as the winter of 1923 (the first issue of *Lef* appeared in March) Brik sought the label and support of Gosizdat. This support was granted, but hesitantly and in a limited manner. In May Gosizdat gave *Lef* its publishing independence, which made things easier organizationally but more difficult financially, since neither *Lef* nor *About That,* produced as a separate booklet, sold well. Later that year Gosizdat again took over publication, and in September of 1923 *Lef* ended its existence as an independent enterprise.

The *Lef* group formed several alliances, with MAPP in 1923 and with the constructivists (Kornely Zelinsky, Ilya Selvinsky, and others) in 1924. In spite of its vociferous insistence on its activist support of the communist regime, it never gained recognition as anything resembling a mouthpiece of the party. In 1924 Trotsky categorically stated that, while the party would not interfere in matters of art, the group around *Lef* definitely had no right to call itself a communist movement. And as early as February of 1925 even Lunacharsky felt obliged to declare *Lef* and its esthetics "obsolete."[1]

But *Lef* and the avant-garde did not capitulate. Many of the ideas of the futurists resurfaced in the declarations and miscellanies of the Literary Center of Constructivists (LTsK), founded in 1924. The fundamental notion advanced by Zelinsky, the theorist of LTsK, was that the growing complexity of modern civilization made it essential to simplify life by using machines in production, and simplified, abstract forms in art. The ideals of constructivism were speed, precision, intensity, and purposefulness. Poetry was seen as an apparatus which worked toward organizing life more rationally. Boris Arvatov's book *Art-Production* (1926), an attempt to fuse a radical formalism with Marxism, viewed art as useful production, maintained that "artistry" amounted to no more and no less than quality of production. This was also Mayakovsky's opinion on this matter, as expressed in "Homeward Bound" (1925), "To Sergey Esenin," and "How to Make Verse" (both 1926). And all this leads directly to the aesthetics of *New Lef* (1927–29).

The key concepts of *New Lef* were the "thingness" (*veshchnost'*) of the work of art; "the literature of fact" (one of its almanacs was entitled *The Literature of Fact: First Miscellany of the Collaborators of Lef,* 1929), or simply "factography"; and a pointed utilitarianism. *New Lef* promoted such genres as the sketch, the travelogue, the diary, and topically "relevant" poetry. The theorists of *New Lef*— Brik, Shklovsky, and Tretyakov—believed that the times of great fictional works were over, and that the future belonged to the newspaper. They particularly approved of film, as the most fact-oriented art form, in the heyday of Dziga Vertov's (1896–1954) documentaries and newsreels. The graphic side of *New Lef* was, accordingly, more subdued than that of *Lef:* standard print without any special attention-catching devices. Mayakovsky expressed the humble, utilitarian aspirations of his art as follows:

> Let poets grumble,
> > swashing their spittle,
> Curling their lips
> > in contempt.
> I, without lowering my soul,
> > shout about things
> which we must have under socialism.
> > ("Let's Have a Material Base!" 1929 [10:149])

Such patent reification of art was bound to clash with Marxism, but certain other aspects of *Lef* aesthetics were in accord with Marxist thought. These included *Lef*'s untiring struggle against art as a social narcotic (in the 1920s the Soviet book market was still flooded with romances, detective stories, and even soft-core pornography). *Lef* was categorically opposed to heroics, high passion, fantastic plots, etc.: "Against Romanticism" was the title of one of Brik's programmatic articles. Even here, *Lef* encountered authoritative opposition. Gorky and Lunacharsky, among others, felt that some revolutionary romanticism, properly channeled, could be useful. On this score, though, *Lef* was in agreement with RAPP, the radical left.

The aesthetics of *Lef* also preached the removal of the personal element, "inner life," and psychology from art. Here Brik and his cohorts stood virtually alone, since even RAPP wanted the typical to be provided with a palpable individuality.

Finally, the aesthetics of *Lef* demanded that the new, revolutionary content of art give birth to new forms as well, and hence *Lef* embraced film, radio, billboard advertising, the mass spectacle, the bulletin board, the political poster, etc. In this respect, too, events were to show that the "old" had more staying power than the theorists of *Lef* thought it did. The novel, the conventional drama, and traditional forms of lyric poetry were far from dead.

The utilitarian, formalist, and rationalist aesthetics of *Lef* and of the Russian formalists is sharply opposed to the organic and intuitive conception of artistic creation which had prevailed in Russia since the days of Vissarion Belinsky (1811–48) and which would soon prevail again. As Andrey Sinyavsky has shown in his celebrated essay "On Socialist Realism" (1959), Mayakovsky's art, as an expression of the aesthetics of *Lef,* shares many positions with seventeenth- and eighteenth-century classicism. Like the latter, it is utilitarian, didactic, and allegoric, and seeks "to instruct (or enlighten) by entertaining."

## The Aesthetics of *Lef*

The contribution of the Russian formalists—especially Viktor Shklovsky and Roman Jakobson—to the aesthetics of *Lef* was significant. The basic theses of formalism are readily recognizable in Mayakovsky's creative practice. The formalists contended that art is essentially craft, technique, and construction, and defined a work of art as the sum of the devices employed in it. They downgraded the direct relevance of the artist's emotional life to his art and scoffed at the notion that a work of art could be born in a flash of inspiration as an "inner vision," whose realization was then a matter of "mere technique." Shklovsky also doubted that a work of art need be an "organic whole," as was previously believed, and suggested instead that while an artist may be guided by a certain theme or plan, he often changes his work, often incorporates into it pieces of his other works, and often abandons one plan for another. The formalists also downgraded the mimetic quality of art and were more interested in the ways in which a work of art differed from nature than resembled it. Shklovsky, in his book *Knight's Move* (1923), called futurism "one of the greatest achievements of human genius" because it fully recognized the absolute independence of the creative imagination.

The formalists preferred works in which a free play of the imagination, deformation of reality (as in the grotesque), "language games," and a liberation of art from its subject matter figured to a high degree. Shklovsky thought "making it strange" (or "defamiliarization") was the basic device of all art. Another device to which he drew attention was "laying bare the device," in an emphatic demonstration that the work at hand is *not* nature or a replica of nature, but a product of human skill. There was a close affinity between formalist thought and the "biomechanics" of Meyerhold, who aimed at transforming his ensemble of actors into a smoothly running machine whose impulses came not "from within" (that is, empathy with roles played), but "from without," as controlled, rhythmically supple, and richly nuanced motion. This demanded acrobatic ability of each individual actor, and what came to be called the "circusization" of the theatre. The constructivist stage sets (by Lyubov Popova and others) of Meyerhold's theater were not designed to resemble a realistic setting of a given play, but instead as a stimulating and challenging environment for the actor, like gymnastic apparatus.

As regards verbal art, the formalist view was that a word is a "thing," subject, of course, to the laws of language and of speech physiology, but not a "shadow," that is, an entity utterly dependent on its social function. Poets, the formalists believed, use words much as other types of artists deal with their material. By becoming conscious of it, the poet "deautomatizes" and "defamiliarizes" the word and, by making the act of its perception "difficult," also involves his audience in this process.

The formalist view of the relationship between art and society was that social stimuli, such as the Revolution, could and should promote changes of form. However, the relationship between art and society had to be consciously determined by the artist, who could let his art serve a political cause, entertainment, enlightenment, or obscurantism.

*Lef,* along with Mayakovsky, by and large subscribed to the formalist view of art. At the same time *Lef*, along with Mayakovsky, were determined to put their art at the service of socialism. They wished to do this knowing that there were other alternatives, specifically entertainment, which, as Mayakovsky said, was "more profitable and prettier." Mayakovsky advertised his utilitarianism in verse as well as in prose, often and persistently. For example, the poem "God's Little Birdie" (1929) described Mayakovsky's encounter with a young poet, a votive of "ce qu'on appelle la poésie." The title alludes to Goethe's ballad "The Singer," in which the singer declares that "he sings like the bird sings," a phrase often quoted in Russian literary criticism. The poem is a mordant satire on *l'art pour l'art*, which makes the poet into a "canary." It concludes: "In our age / he is a poet, // he / is a writer, / who is useful. // Put away this piece of pastry! / Give me some verse / which will help us to get some bread. // In our day / he is a writer // who writes / a march / or a slogan!" (10:113).

Mayakovsky scoffed at "objective" literature and prided himself on being a "tendentious realist." When Jean Cocteau told him that the French had no literary "schools," but were free individualists, Mayakovsky commented that this was "anything but a mark of the superiority of the French spirit, but simply 'political darkness,' in which all cats are grey" (4:231), a sign not of progress, but of decadence. Mayakovsky did not want literature to occupy its own little niche. Rather, he wanted it to be "on every page of the daily newspaper, or not at all"; he wanted it to be part of the main fare, not a "dessert."

The element of constructivism is strong in Mayakovsky, emerging in his verse as well as in his theoretical prose. Mayakovsky's interest was in the manufactured, produced *thing*. Pasternak's conception of the poet as a sponge soaking up life's experience was quite alien to Mayakovsky, who said that he had "grown a brain / not to smell / but to invent roses" ("The Fifth Internationale," 1922 {4:107}). In "Brooklyn Bridge" (1925), Mayakovsky exalts the engineer at the expense of the artist, and "construction" at the expense of "style."

On the other hand, Mayakovsky was too much an artist of the prerevolutionary avant-garde not to love the excitement of creating new forms for their own sake. The poem "Verlaine and Cézanne" (1925), from his Parisian cycle, eloquently expresses his sense of belonging to the international avant-garde, his exhilaration at breathing the free air of Paris, and his contempt for the institutionalized art of the Association of Artists of Revolutionary Russia (AKhRR) back in the Soviet Union. While Mayakovsky was willing to write "to order" (upon a "social commission," as the saying went at the time), he insisted on freedom to determine the form of his work. To the very end, Mayakovsky's verses—including purely propaganda verses—retained their futurist flair, even with an occasional dash of cubism. He felt that he as author, as the one who faced his audience, must decide whether his work was "intelligible" and had the proper effect.

Mayakovsky formulated his aesthetics of the *Lef* period brilliantly in his essay "How to Make Verse," an account of how he wrote "To Sergey Esenin." It may be likened to Edgar Allan Poe's essay "The Philosophy of Composition" describing the genesis of "The Raven." Mayakovsky establishes that the "social commission" should supersede the poet's private persona, but he also makes an eloquent plea for professionalism in poetry. The occasion for writing a poem is one thing, but its actual genesis is something different. It is born as an indistinct rhythmic rumble: "Rhythm is the basic power, the basic energy of verse. It cannot be explained, one can talk about it the way one talks about magnetism or electricity" (12:101) (in 1926, a layman would know of magnetism and electricity only that they are "forces"). However, Mayakovsky rejects any conception of poetry as mere "word magic," that is, the acoustic side of verse as an end in itself. Rather, he seeks to impart to acoustic elements a function linking them to the poem's message. For example, he points out how he uses alliteration for emphasis and how he avoids too striking rhymes at certain junctures so as not to divert the reader's attention from a crucial point.

In drawing conclusions from his practical experience, Mayakovsky maintains that poetry is "production, difficult, very complicated, but production" (12:116). Making verse requires study, expertise, the acquisition of certain work habits, and ought to be approached professionally, like all production. The poet ought to work at his job daily. Only a professional attitude will allow the poet continually to come up with new material and new devices, something essential to his maintaining the high quality of his work. Mayakovsky claims, furthermore, that in order to understand his social commission correctly, the poet must himself be in the focus of public life, and a progressive member of his class. Also, "a good notebook and skill in using it are more important than an ability to write flawless verse in dead meters."

## Mayakovsky and Painting

Mayakovsky had started out as a painter. During the Civil War he had devoted as much time to drawing cartoons and posters as to writing poetry. Actively interested in film as far back as 1913, he had given much of the year 1918 over to writing film scenarios and playing the lead in his own films. These interests continued even during the last seven years of his life. Upon his return in 1923 from his first visit to western Europe, Mayakovsky signed a contract with Gosizdat to write a booklet entitled "A Seven Day Review of French Painting." Mayakovsky submitted a twenty-page typescript with clippings from Paris newspapers and ten color and fifteen black-and-white illustrations, but the booklet was not printed during Mayakovsky's lifetime. In it we meet an art critic who reports on art which he has known for years. Picasso, Braque, Delaunay, Derain, Matisse, and others, he says, are doing essentially the same things they were doing before the war. Mayakovsky maintains that now it is from Russia that the last word of art has come: constructivism, though "not the constructivism of artists who from good and much needed wire and sheet metal make unnecessary constructions, but a constructivism which conceives of the artist's formal work as of an engineering detail, required to give shape to all of our practical life" (4:238).

Mayakovsky's description of the fall salon is witty without being amateurish. Here, for example, is his description of the one picture that draws crowds:

This is number 870, a nude by the Japanese artist Fujita. A sprawling lady with her hands under her head. Naked. The lady's armpits are wide open. In her armpits there are little hairs. And it is the hairs that attract all this attention. These little hairs are done with shocking conscientiousness. Not with any kind of general smear, but each separately. So you can get yourself a receipt with their exact number from the Central Bristle Co. Not one will get lost, they've all been counted. (4:239)

The article contains separate notes on Picasso, Delaunay, and Léger. Mayakovsky analyzes the work of each from the viewpoint of its revolutionary potential, and yet succeeds in saying some interesting things, as, for instance, on Picasso:

In his jumping from one device to the other, one must see not the artist's departure [from cubist analysis of nature], but rather the lunging, to this side or the other, of an artist who has already reached the limit of formal accomplishment in a given manner and who now searches for a way to apply what he knows to some end, but can't, in an atmosphere of stuffy French reality. (4:246)

Mayakovsky found Delaunay and Léger more receptive to revolutionary ideas, that is, the idea of placing their art at the service of the world revolution. He considered Braque the least progressive of the cubists: In him, he says, "the temper of revolutionary French cubism is pressed into proper forms, agreeable to all"—"a balancing act between the salon and art, though performed, to give credit where credit is due, with great taste" (4:248).

In discussing his old friends Larionov and Goncharova, by then resident in Paris, Mayakovsky praises their positive attitude toward communist Russia above all else. One senses that Mayakovsky is anxiously reassuring his reader and himself that "a revolutionary in the field of art will remain one to the end" (4:250). Mayakovsky's conclusions from his Parisian impressions are noteworthy. He theorizes that the beginning of the twentieth century was devoted to "the solution of purely formal problems" (4:251) and that this work had been completed by 1915, so that art was then once more at a crossroads: it could either adapt its formal innovations to bourgeois tastes or use them to create a new social environment in workers' clubs, libraries, and other public buildings. In this sense, Mayakovsky concludes, Soviet art is the leader of world art, even though technically it has much to learn from the French.

Mayakovsky never abandoned these ideas, which were also largely those of the constructivist aesthetics of *New Lef*. The sets for Mayakovsky's plays *The Bedbug* and *The Bathhouse* were done in a strictly constructivist style. It was just as natural that the sets for the utopian second act of *The Bedbug* should have been done by Mayakovsky's old constructivist collaborator, Rodchenko, as it was for Meyerhold to stage the play and for Shostakovich to compose the music for it.

## Mayakovsky and Film

Mayakovsky's early and constant love for the cinema was an unhappy one. He had the talent to become a great filmmaker, but was never involved in even a good one. Mayakovsky correctly saw the potential of the silent film, not only as a way to bring the theater to more people, but also as an avenue to a new theater that would overcome the "naive realism of Chekhov and Gorky." The films Mayakovsky made in 1918 hardly justified such a prognosis. His long poems—*War and the World, Man, About That,*—were infinitely better realizations of a cinematic imagination than these films were, and he himself called them "sentimental trash made to order." In the 1920s Western films were still shown in Russia quite indiscriminately, and so Mayakovsky was always abreast of the latest developments. An interesting 100-line poem, "Film Air" (1923), is a tribute to Charlie Chaplin, whom Mayakovsky greets as an ally against the bourgeois world.

In the winter of 1926–27 Mayakovsky prepared a collection of his film scenarios for publication. His preface lists a total of eleven, of which the first five have been lost. (Subsequently Mayakovsky wrote three more scenarios, none of which was made into a film.) The preface also suggests that the scenarios *Heart of Cinema* and *Shkafolyubov's Love* were "typical of his work, and of interest as steps toward a new cinematography." *Heart of Cinema*, a new version of Mayakovsky's earlier scenario *Fettered by Film*, was regrettably never made into a film. It shows Mayakovsky in full and imaginative command of all the techniques of silent film which had been developed to a high level by such directors as Eisenstein, Vertov, Lev Kuleshov, and Vsevolod Pudovkin. Mayakovsky consistently emphasizes devices intrinsic to film: montage, stills, accelerated motion, angled views, and such. The plot of *Heart of Cinema* is about a painter's love for a beautiful film star. Its cinematic point is that the film star alternates between a two- and a three-dimensional existence. She steps out of a film screen to join the painter, but when at his place, needs a screen on the wall to materialize. There are many other ingenious effects (the fact that the hero is a painter leads to some good ones) in this scenario, and in Mayakovsky's other scenarios. Mayakovsky's almost total lack of success in film must be attributed to the fact that by the time he got seriously interested in it the period of free experimentation (which included "absolute" or "nonobjective" film) was over in the Soviet Union. Also, his whimsical and witty scenarios must have posed a technical challenge which Soviet film studios became less and less interested in meeting as time passed.

## The Practice of Practical Poetry

Starting in 1925, Mayakovsky wrote a great deal of poetry for children, much of it technically excellent—its rhythms are just as lively and its rhymes just as fresh as those of his best poetry for adults—and all of it aggressively didactic. He instructs Soviet children to be neat, to do their lessons, not to bully their smaller schoolmates, and also to stay away from religion: "This is a church, / god's temple, // here / old women / come in the morning. // They made themselves a picture, / called it 'god,' // and wait / for this god to help them. // They sure are stupid— / no way / the picture will help them" ("We Take a Walk," 1925).

The lengthy "Tale about Petya, a Fat Child, and Sima, a Thin One" (1925), written in the meter of Pushkin's famous fairy tales (trochaic tetrameter), is a rather nasty propaganda piece. Petya, the fat boy, whose father is a bourgeois and a wealthy shopkeeper, has only bad qualities: he is greedy, he overeats, he is stupid and lazy, and he mistreats animals. Sima, son of a factory worker, is intelligent, neat, hard working, and he protects animals. In the end, each gets his reward. Petya bursts in half, spilling out all kinds of goodies which Sima and his proletarian friends then happily consume.

Mayakovsky's best known piece for children is a rousing march calling on Russia's young pioneers (members of the communist youth organization for children nine to fourteen years of age) to join rifle clubs, so that they may be prepared to defend their country. That children of that age group should sing "Let's take our new rifles, / with flags on their bayonets" is perfectly understandable considering the fact that Soviet school curricula include compulsory military training.

A considerable portion of Mayakovsky's work was devoted to outright commercial art and verse, and to the composition and illustration of public service messages. The latter dealt with a variety of subjects, such as confiscation of church property, the fuel crisis, transportation, labor discipline, prompt payment of taxes, and hygiene. For example, Mayakovsky authored jingles such as "Clean your teeth daily, / morning and night!"; "Don't be afraid of water, / wash every day!"; or, in a less harmless vein: "We'll kick out / the absentee-churchgoer! // Don't mix factory whistle / and church bells!" Mayakovsky was also good at concocting slogans for Mayday and October Revolution rallies, such as "Lenin's banner / is always with us!"—all of this properly rhymed, of course.

Much of Mayakovsky's work was outright advertising, which he took seriously, insisting that it was every bit as important as his other work (see his article, "Propaganda and Advertising," 1923). Mayakovsky authored "odes" and "ballads" promoting government bond issues and lotteries. He urged women to buy the simple and loose dresses of the state operated factory rather than the "latest fashion" at private shops. He invited "proletarians to visit the Moscow planetarium." He wrote advertising lines in verse and in prose, and often made the drawings, too, selling journals, pencils, galoshes, textiles, tea, produce, and many other items. He designed caramel wrappers promoting the metric system and the Red Army. In the West an advertising man of his talent and productivity would have made a fortune.

Mayakovsky stated and practiced the utilitarian aesthetics of *Lef* in a huge output of versified pieces which showed that he was no mere "fellow traveler" (a label he always angrily rejected) but a mouthpiece of the communist regime. As he put it in "Don't Get Carried Away" (1929): "If your / name is 'cow,' // you / must have / milk / and an udder. // But if you are / without milk / and without udder, // what the hell's the use / of your bovine name? // This / is also true of the artist / and the poet" (10:155). As to the fate of the artist's individuality under such circumstances, Mayakovsky had no illusions: "Huge superproblems, / huger than elephants, // must be solved / by our country / of millions of brains. // Meanwhile / individuals / walk on the side, / having // their own / separate opinion about everything" (10:138). The poem, entitled "A Separate Opinion" (1929), ends with these words: "Don't stick / any wedges / into our job— // we / and the masses / have the same ideas // and the same / Party line" (10:140).

The commentary to Mayakovsky's *Collected Works* suggests that his "occasional poetry"—which represents the bulk of his production—was often, and perhaps always, directly consonant with the official party policies of the moment. Much of this poetry appeared on the pages of the party press. Much of it was linked to the editorial and news sections of the periodicals in which it appeared. Many of Mayakovsky's poems were dedicated to meetings of the party and its affiliated organizations, congresses, and conventions of the international communist movement, to holidays in the political calendar ("Armed Forces Day," Mayday, and such), and various festive occasions, such as sports festivals, antiwar rallies, Aviation Day, or the conferring of the Order of the Red Banner on the Leningrad Komsomol. These poems earned Mayakovsky the label of a "writer of odes" *(odopisets),* the Soviet equivalent of a court poet who celebrates royal birthdays, weddings, victories, and anniversaries in congratulatory verse.

Mayakovsky's utilitarian repertory was, however, very broad. A great deal of his poetry is straightforwardly didactic, and covers every imaginable facet of Soviet life. We hear Mayakovsky promoting a campaign against drunkenness, swearing, and other "uncultured" habits ("Why?" 1928). We hear him urge housewives to quit their kitchens and opt for factory cafeterias ("A Most Important Bit of Advice to a Housewife," 1928), advise peasants to plant more beets, carrots, and turnips ("Peasant Affairs," 1924), expatiate on the usefulness of rural correspondents ("The Rural Correspondent," 1924), encourage citizens to open a savings account ("To Avoid Intellectual Controversy," 1928), and discourage the perilous practice of jaywalking ("On Pedestrians and Jaywalkers," 1928). Not all his diatribes may seem trivial to the Western reader: for example, Mayakovsky was consistent in denouncing anti-Semitism in truly

impassioned invective, as in "Yid" (1928), where he urges Russians
to eliminate the word "Yid" *(zhid)* from their language:

> This word
> > is a password
> > > for priests,
> > > > for nuns,
> recruited from among countesses we neglected to hang.
> > > > > > (9:117)

In many of his poems Mayakovsky appears as a moralist, denouncing nepotism and corruption; hooligans who molest bypassers,
insult women, and use foul language in public ("Hooligans," 1924);
absenteeism ("Hey, Worker!" 1924); drunkenness, especially on
holidays ("Whose Holidays?" 1928); gambling ("Red Arabs," 1928);
prostitution ("Help!" 1924); and other social evils. Mayakovsky,
himself a moderate social drinker, particularly detested drunkenness.
He presented this vice as a vestige of the old order, and blamed
Christian holidays and family customs, as well as enemies of the
regime who purposely subverted Soviet society by producing and
selling liquor illegally, for its continued prevalence (see "Down with
the Whites and the Greens," 1928). In a poem of 1929, "Two
Opiates," Mayakovsky exclaims:

> Throw out
> > from your life
> > > two opiates:
> God
> > and alcohol!
> > (10:93)

A good many of Mayakovsky's didactic poems incorporate outright antireligious propaganda, much of it of a mean and nasty kind.
His relatively few pieces devoted to national and international relations are not very pleasant reading either. Where nationality was
concerned, Mayakovsky preached more or less the official line: all
nationalities are to be respected, but Russian, the language of Lenin,
is of course the most important: a Negro, even if he were advanced
in age, still ought to learn Russian, because it was the language of
Lenin ("To Our Youth," 1927). As for international relations, Mayakovsky never hesitated to propound the most outrageous lies of

Soviet propaganda. He makes a nasty response to foreign "allegations" that there is no freedom of speech in the Soviet Union ("Ivan Ivanovich Gonorarchikov," 1927). He consistently denounces the Western powers as warmongers and enemies of humanity (see "Bonebreakers and Butchers," 1928), and also holds them responsible for certain internal troubles of the Soviet Union: "Now, / from verbal rubbish, // the government / of British blockheads // has proceeded / to terror: // Upon our / territory // they have unleashed their band / / of spies, / arsonists, / bandits, / and murderers . . ." (8:135) and so forth, in the same vein ("Appeal," 1927). In those years the Western powers, and Britain in particular, were often accused of criminal sabotage of the Soviet economy, terrorist acts, and other wrecking activities allegedly carried out by their paid agents. Mayakovsky also followed the party line in denouncing such Western socialists as Ramsay MacDonald quite as viciously as he did their conservative opponents (see "To the British Worker," 1926).

But most of all, Mayakovsky led the chorus backing the incipient industrialization of Russia and Stalin's first Five-Year Plan. Mayakovsky committed himself to "production literature" ahead of almost everyone else. A lengthy poem of 1923, "To the Workers of Kursk, who Produced the First Iron Ore, a Temporary Monument by the Hand of Vladimir Mayakovsky," contains a lecture on geology and paleontology, a description of the first drillings, and an enthusiastic prognosis for the future, and ends in a panegyric to the working men and women of Kursk. Later Mayakovsky wrote poems on the construction of hydroelectric plants, metallurgical plants, the Moscow subway, and other projects. His exhortations always reflected the official propaganda of the period. His "March of Shock Brigades" (1930) was a response to the formation of shock worker brigades a few months earlier. His warnings that the pace of production must be kept up without loss of quality ("Alarm," 1930) echoed those published in editorials all over the country. When "socialist competition" was introduced, Mayakovsky dutifully contrasted the evils of competition in capitalist countries with the benefits of "creative competition" in the U.S.S.R. ("Two Competitions," 1929). Last but not least, the slogan "The Five-Year Plan in Four Years!" also reverberates in Mayakovsky's verses (see "The First Five," 1929). Mayakovsky supported the ruthless collectivization of agriculture with no less enthusiasm than the Five-Year Plan. His "March of the Twenty-Five Thousand" (1930), occasioned by a decree of the

Central Committee of the Communist party mobilizing 25,000 communist organizers to speed up collectivization, has a cruel ring:

> The enemy is advancing,
>                         it is time to finish off
>     their band
>         of priests and *kulaks*.
>
> (10:177)

While Mayakovsky's hatred of the bourgeois seems to have been deep and genuine, his image of the *kulak* is that of Stalin's propaganda, vicious and false.

## Vladimir Ilich Lenin

Mayakovsky's verse epics *Vladimir Ilich Lenin* (1924, almost 3,000 lines) and *Good! An October Poem* (1927, over 3,000 lines) are considered by Soviet critics to be Mayakovsky's most important works. Both fall well within the classicist genre of the historical-didactic epic, with a panegyric strain also in evidence, particularly in *V. I. Lenin*. Their style alternates between the folksiness of satire and anecdote, the soberly prosaic approach of instruction and reportage, emotion-laden lyricism, and high-flown rhetoricism. The poet's persona disappears, most of the time, behind the impersonal voice of a Party activist at an indoctrination seminar. He perceives his audience as perhaps a notch above the wholly uneducated masses, the presumed addressee of much of Mayakovsky's propaganda verse: they are semiliterate party cadres, maybe, familiar with the basics of Marxist-Leninist doctrine and now taking a refresher course.

In an editorial note in *Lef* entitled "Don't Do Business with Lenin!"[2] (written soon after Lenin's death), Mayakovsky had denounced the commercial distribution of gypsum busts of Lenin by Gosizdat. The note was almost immediately vetoed by the authorities and removed. Lars Kleberg has suggested that the poet may have actually been addressing a warning to himself: Lenin could become an object of worship, a cult figure, and his living memory and living thoughts might be lost.[3] (This did in fact happen almost immediately.)[4] *V. I. Lenin* is first and foremost a vivid account of recent history, simplified and expressed in figurative language, for example, "Capitalism grew fat / like a biblical cow / or ox, // licking its chops. / Its tongue is called parliament" (6:247). Or, "Capital-

ism / grew mightily, // a porcupine of contradictions, / and ever
stronger, / with bayonets for quills" (6:256). In a brief survey of
the principles of Marxism-Leninism (a triumph of didactic poetry!),
Mayakovsky manages to find rhymes for "Marx," "publicism," "capitalist," and even "surplus value." His account of World War I,
the Revolution, Civil War, NEP, and Lenin's illness and death is
fairly accurate. The leader's journey from Zurich to the Finland
Station in Petrograd in a sealed car provided by the German government is mentioned, with proper excuses. The events of 25 October 1917 are described as if Mayakovsky had witnessed them.
Embarrassingly, Trotsky and Zinovev, later to become unpersons,
are given prominent mention, though so is Stalin. The inglorious
peace treaty of Brest-Litovsk is brought up with proper apologies,
and Mayakovsky defends Lenin's controversial policies, such as the
launching of the NEP, in the proper terms.

Interspersed with "history," one finds a good deal of comic relief—at the expense of the class enemy, of course:

> The capitalist
> > sells
> > > old women
> holes
> > made by the nails
> > > of Our Lord's cross,
> and feathers
> > from the tail
> > > of the Holy Ghost.
> > > (6:248)

Time and again Mayakovsky lapses into futuristic language games.
The lines, "All around, / with faces that will serve equally well //
as faces / or as buttocks, // there's buttockfaced police," are enhanced
by a cubist sound pattern: "s *lits*óm, / chto rávno go*dít*sya // byt' i
*lits*óm / i yágo*ditsey*, // za*dolíts*aya po*líts*iya" (6:247).

But there is also the sublime side of the poem, arranged in a
hierarchy of themes: humanity, the proletariat, the party, Lenin.
The poet brings the humanity and humanism of Lenin and his fellow
communists to the fore time and again. Lenin is "the most human
of men" ("samy chelovechny chelovek"). The world's grief at Lenin's
death is an expression of the solidarity of the working class: "One
could not partake / more strongly, / more purely // of that great

and noble feeling / whose name is / class!" (6:304). The poem is dedicated to the Russian Communist party—Lenin's party: "We say Lenin, / and by that we mean / the party, // we say / the party, / and by that we mean: / Lenin" (6:267). The poem features an inspired sermon on the glories of the party, introduced by the lines, "I want to / make it shine more, / that noblest of words, / the party" (6:265). The poem also has its cosmic moments: "Before me / looms / in an aura of red banners, // dark, / immobile, / the globe of the earth. // Above the world, a coffin, / immobile and mute" (6:306).

*V. I. Lenin* contains many ingenious conceits. Carefully versified and rhymed, it contains a great deal of judiciously placed sound symbolism. Obviously Mayakovsky did the best job he could with it. This, combined with the poem's indubitable ideological rectitude, makes it surprising that *V. I. Lenin* met with a hesitant reception. Readers generally felt that it was too cerebral, not a sincere expression of emotion. By the time the poem acquired the stature it has today, Lenin had long since become a myth, and worse yet, an official myth. *V. I. Lenin* was declared a classic without ever having reached a live audience. Current Soviet comments that the poem "is characterized by a monumental power of sociohistorical generalization and philosophic harmony" are the kind of praise accorded to dead classics.[5] *V. I. Lenin,* for all the poet's honest effort, was a stillborn work.

### Good!

*Good!* is less ambitious and more successful. If *V. I. Lenin* was Mayakovsky's attempt at writing "big history," *Good!* is essentially an excursion into "little history." Like *V. I. Lenin,* it combines the satirical with the heroic, but the satirical element is more prominent. The poem tells the story of the October Revolution, beginning with a masterful dramatic description of unrest sweeping the country under Kerensky's Provisional Government. There follows a mock-heroic lampoon of Kerensky as a vain actor playing the role of Napoleon—badly, in a travesty utilizing the rhythm and intonation of Lermontov's romantic poem "The Aerial Ship," devoted to the legend of Napoleon. There follows yet another parody, a reenactment of the scene in Pushkin's *Eugene Onegin* where Tatyana confesses her love for Onegin to her old nurse. S. D. Kuskova, a Social Democrat who turned her back on the Bolsheviks, is Tatyana; P. N. Milyukov, leader of the Constitutional Democrat party, is the nurse; and Kerensky is now Onegin. After yet another satirical dialogue between two officers discussing the unthinkable—Lenin, that troublemaker, prime minister? Lyovka Bronstein [Trotsky] in command of Russian officers?—there comes a magnificent, somberly exultant account of the storming of the Winter Palace and the fall of the Provisional Government. The passage is one of Mayakovsky's finest achievements.

The next episode is the first to adopt a personal point of view. One night, at an hour "when only poets and thieves are in the streets," Mayakovsky passes by one of the fires lit by soldiers along the Neva River and recognizes one of the soldiers warming himself there: he is Aleksandr Blok, the great symbolist poet, whose world is collapsing around him. He has just received word that his library has been burned at his country estate.

> Blok stood and stared
>                and Blok's shadow
> stared, too,
>         rising on a wall . . .
> As though
>      both
>          were waiting for Christ
> to come walking across the water.
> But Christ
>      had no intention
>          of showing himself to Blok.
>              (8:266)

Here Mayakovsky mockingly alludes to the concluding line of Blok's poem *The Twelve* (1918), which describes Jesus Christ leading a patrol of red guards. Instead of Christ, Mayakovsky has a crowd of factory hands and day laborers marching across Russia, taking over factories and estates, wreaking revenge on their oppressors: "Perish— / what's old. // Smash it / to pieces. // Beat / the bosses! // Bang! / Bang!" (8:267).

The next several episodes describe life in the young Soviet Republic, counterrevolution, foreign intervention, economic collapse, cold and hunger, with a couple of episodes presented from the angle of Mayakovsky's personal experiences in freezing and starving Moscow of that time. Then Mayakovsky returns to history to describe the attempt on Lenin's life on 30 August 1918, the subsequent proclamation of Red terror, and the final onslaught of the Whites, with a detailed description of the evacuation of General Wrangel's army from the Crimea. The poem ends with a hymn to the future of the Soviet Republic, an eulogy of the communist heroes who died in the Revolution, and a solemn peroration in praise of the wonderful young country which is the poet's home.

*Good!* is probably Mayakovsky's best poetic work about the Revolution, but it is very uneven. It contains magnificent epic passages and some good realistic descriptions, but several of its episodes are no more than versified feuilletons. The versification is perhaps not quite so polished as that of *V. I. Lenin.*

Two themes of Mayakovsky's civic poetry seem to have been closer to his heart than all the rest: his struggle with Soviet bureaucrats and with Soviet philistines. To be sure, Mayakovsky's seemingly bold attacks on inefficiency and corruption in the Soviet bureaucracy were merely versified versions of editorials or feuilletons in the party press, but still some of them must have made him enemies, for example, "The Coward" (1928), directed against Soviet citizens who will not speak their minds out of cowardice or for personal advantage. And Mayakovsky's persistent and vitriolic satires directed against a good Soviet citizen's pursuit of modest bourgeois comforts must have cut many readers to the quick. Many must have resented his poem "Let's Vote 'Uninterrupted' " (1929), in which he denounced holidays as orgies of superstition, drunkenness, and family fights, and proposed doing away with all holidays and introducing a seven-day work week, with workers getting their day off on different days. (This was not Mayakovsky's idea, of course, but the government's, which introduced such a system on 29 August 1929.) When Mayakovsky denounced the return of bourgeois fashions to Soviet clothing stores ("A Poem on Clothes and Youth," 1930) or bad movies, whose harmfulness he likened to that of vodka ("Cinema and Vodka," 1928), he was well within the bounds of routine editorial opinion. But when he suggested that one might invent "an universal powder / that would at once / kill / bedbugs and philistines" ("A Rime about Trash and Petty Trash," 1928), he may have gone too far, for by then the Soviet philistine was quickly coming into his own.

## The Travel Poetry

Some of Mayakovsky's most interesting poetry and prose was written as a result of his frequent trips to the West. Mayakovsky was only one of many twentieth-century Russian writers who wrote important pieces on foreign themes, but Mayakovsky took a different approach to them. While the symbolists still sustained the myth—created by Belinsky and canonized by Dostoevsky—which held that the Russian genius, capable of assimilating the creations of all Western nations, would also create a new synthesis of all of them, Mayakovsky viewed himself strictly as the Soviet Union's roving ambassador: "I / am the Soviet ambassador of verse, / and my country / and I // throw down the gauntlet / to your measly States." In this poem ("A Challenge," 1925), one of Mayakovsky's "America" cycle, he goes on to challenge American puritanism (he will "kiss—unlawfully—their long-legged wives"), prohibition (he will have his "White Horse" every afternoon), and even the almighty dollar. He renews the challenge in one of his later poems "Americans are Surprised" (1929):

> As for your
> > fleet-footed
> > > famous America,
> we shall catch up with her
> > > and overtake her!
> > > (10:90)

Mayakovsky's challenge is present in virtually every poem of the foreign cycles. As early as "The Fifth Internationale" (1922), Mayakovsky prophesies the takeover of Poland by the Soviet Union and a Red Germany; he also calls Latvia "half a Russian province." Mayakovsky's frequent anti-Polish sorties accurately reflected the attitude of the Soviet government, as did his anti-British tirades. The poems of his Parisian cycle contain numerous allusions to a coming revolution: "It would be good / to sweep these shanties / into a museum! // Ought to have here / a steel / and glass / palace for workers, / accommodating millions" (6:218) (the "shanties" here are the royal palaces of Versailles) ("Versailles," 1925). In "Notre Dame" (1925), Mayakovsky reflects on what will happen to that cathedral when "the workers have stormed police headquarters across the square." And even Mayakovsky's Parisian love poem, "Letter to Tatyana Yakovleva" (1928), concludes with these lines:

> I'll
>> take you
>>> anyway, some day,
>> you alone,
>>> or you and Paris.
>>>> (9:389)

Even though Mayakovsky obviously enjoyed his stays in Paris, in America, and elsewhere in the West, he still looked for openings for his communist propaganda line more than for anything else. Certainly the beauties of Western culture did not attract him: "Verses on the Beauties of Architecture" (1928) is a ballad about a building in Paris which collapsed, killing thirty workers.

Mayakovsky wrote a number of poems with an anticolonialist message, including several in the "America" cycle ("Black and White," "Syphilis," "Christopher Columbus," all 1925). Their message follows the familiar propaganda track: greedy, brutal, and lecherous white capitalists exploiting—economically, physically, sexually—honest, hard-working, but naive colored people, who are, however, awakening under the leadership of the Comintern and letting their oppressors know that the end of their reign is near:

> They are waiting.
>> Comintern, translate
> racial hatred
>> into class hatred.
>>> ("I testify," 1926 [7:61])

Mayakovsky's cycle *Verses about America* (1925–26), containing some twenty poems, most of them quite long, exemplifies his artistic power. The ideological core of Mayakovsky's image of America is that, on the positive side, America's "futurism of naked technology" has overcome the stagnating rural mentality of the past; but that, on the negative side, the ethical and aesthetic aspects of American life have remained backward: "I meant to advance / seven thousand miles, // and arrived seven years back" ("The Skyscraper: A Cross-Section," 1925 [7:69]). In "The Miss and Woolworth's" (1925), the poet stands before a Woolworth's display window to address a

girl demonstrating a new knife sharpener. He tells her the truth
about her exploitation, in Russian, but she thinks he is a young
executive, or even a millionaire living in the building's penthouse
and hears instead sweet English phrases, promises of love and mar-
riage. The exasperated poet asks: "Where could I get a knife to
carve / into her head / the idea // that Russians have another way /
for workers to get to / all the floors, // without dreams, / without
weddings, / without waiting for an inheritance" (7:65).

Mayakovsky's American cityscapes, both in poetry ("Broadway,"
"Brooklyn Bridge") and prose, are masterful. In a prose sketch of
Chicago he quotes Carl Sandburg's poem extensively, comments on
it, and then expands it to put forth more facts about Chicago's
industrial might.

While he makes fun of the Americanized Russian idiom of his
émigré hosts, Mayakovsky himself incorporates scores of American
words into his poems, finding rhymes for "avenue," "street," "lift,"
"Coolidge," "chewing gum," "money," "dollar," "business," "subway," "elevator," "Hudson," "Maxwell coffee," and "good to the
last drop." To be sure, he can write distortions about things in
American life that were hateful to him: "A Decent Citizen," one
of his angrier poems, describes, among other things, the exploitation
of consumptive garment workers, a sleazy boss pawing at a working
girl's breasts, a band of "sexless old hags" tarring and feathering a
prostitute, the Salvation Army, club-wielding police, the "Democrat" Coolidge, and—in a crowning effect—the Statue of Liberty
transferred to Ellis Island, "as a guardian of hypocrisy, cents, and
lard."

However, the best verses of Mayakovsky's "America" cycle follow
the line of his utopian and cosmic imagination. "Brooklyn Bridge"
(1925), ostensibly an ode to human skill and ingenuity, really views
the bridge, "quite a thing" though it may be, as no more than a
promise of far greater things to come. Significantly, the poet imagines himself an archaeologist of the distant future who reconstructs
our fledgling civilization from the remains of Brooklyn Bridge,
much as we now reconstruct dinosaurs from a few odd bones. "Camp
*Nit Gedajge*" (1925), whose trochaic hexameter (with caesura after
the third foot) offers what may be Mayakovsky's most irresistible
rhythm, is ostensibly about Young Communists at summer camp
on the Hudson, "whose song / makes / the Hudson flow into the

Moscow river." But it is even more about Mayakovsky's—and mankind's—eternal dream of mastering the movement of time.

## Proletarian Utopianism

Though Mayakovsky's utopian fantasy is best known from his plays, his poetry also contains many utopian motifs, and the point of view in many of his poems is wholly or partly one of the future, as in *War and the World, Man,* and *About That.* Two less well-known epic poems—*The Fifth Internationale* (1922, close to 1,000 lines) and *The Flying Proletarian* (1925, 1,860 lines)—belong almost entirely to the utopian genre, as the poet duly acknowledges in *The Fifth Internationale* when he announces: "Here it is, / Life, // dreamed of since the days of Fourier, / Robert Owen and Saint-Simon" (4:134). The poem is a rather disorganized mixture of playful conceits, short range dreams of economic progress (by 1925–30, he says, swampy farms, wooden plows, and leaky roofs will have been replaced by "red and green roofs, tractors, drained fields, and happy peasants"), and cosmic adventure. On a flight through twenty-two dimensions of space (Mayakovsky mentions Einstein), the poet contends with the loss of his familiar solid body by forging a structure of thought that will "metallize the spirit," and then converts one of his organs after another into a machine. His ear becomes a superreceiver of cosmic waves (have we not heard of this in Pushkin's poem "The Prophet"?) and he speaks from a cosmic vantage point where the earth appears like a drop of water under a microscope. There is the globe: the U.S.S.R. glowing red, Poland barely pieced together from scraps, America all dark, here and there flashes of revolutionary activity. He then has the satisfaction of seeing the five-pointed star spread all over the globe so that the whole world, Sahara and all, is converted into a flowering garden.

*The Flying Proletarian,* set in the year 2125, features a giant air battle, with death rays and such, between the Soviet proletarian and the American bourgeois air forces. The latter prevails until an uprising of New York workers against their government turns the tide. Mayakovsky's communist future is all comfort and electric ease: electric razors, electric toothbrushes, everybody with his own private airplane (Moscow no longer has any streets, just airports). Labor is wholly mechanized, so that a worker merely operates a keyboard. Altogether, Mayakovsky's utopia is written from the viewpoint of a laborer who is tired of backbreaking, dirty work. Mayakovsky holds that work should be easy and clean, but says nothing about its being interesting. There are no kitchens, no housework. People eat in aerocafeterias and amuse themselves with cosmic cinemas, cosmic dances, and such—all nonalcoholic (alcohol is served by prescription only). The sport of the future is avio-polo—soccer has long since been abandoned as crude and boring.

## The Plays

Mayakovsky's plays *The Bedbug* and *The Bathhouse* are a quintessential expression of the poet's futurist imagination, and should be seen in the context of his futurist aesthetics. Much as "the word in itself" was a cornerstone of futurist poetics, so "the theater as such" was a cornerstone of the modernist theater for which Mayakovsky wrote his plays. The theater of Nikolay Evreinov and Vsevolod Meyerhold was based on the notion that the theater should not present simulations of "real life" (as did Stanislavsky's Moscow Art Theater), but function as a structure in itself, through which the playwright could make statements about "real life." Mayakovsky's plays were well suited to the virtuosic and nimble puppets of Meyerhold's "biomechanics"; They fell flat when staged in a conventional "psychological" manner.

Mayakovsky knew perfectly well what he wanted to give his audience: "Instead of psychological theater, we give the public our spectacular {*zrelishchny*, from *zrelishche*, "spectacle"] theater," he said in a public discussion on *The Bathhouse* on 27 March 1930. He also said that his play should be propaganda, and since nobody denied that his stage was an "arena reflecting political slogans," the only real question was whether it satisfied its other purpose—to be an amusing spectacle. If Moscow workers, as quoted by the press, said that *The Bathhouse* was a "circus farce," or a "Punch-and-Judy show," or that it was "unartistic," this indicated to Mayakovsky that they had seen the show exactly as he wished. He admitted, though, that mistakes had occurred. For one thing, the theater was not spacious enough for the play to be a real mass spectacle. Nevertheless, the fact remained that *The Bathhouse* was a flop and *The Bedbug* was not a great hit. The fact that both plays scored huge successes after 1953 may indicate that the audiences of 1929–30 were not ready for Mayakovsky's and Meyerhold's theater.

*The Bedbug: A Fantastic Comedy in Nine Pictures* (1928–29) is a play in two acts. The first act features a Soviet version of Molière's *Le Bourgeois gentilhomme*. Ivan Prisypkin (Powders), a proletarian purged from the party but with a genuine union card, has decided to reap the fruits of the Revolution now. He has abandoned his proletarian girl friend Zoya, who shoots herself (not fatally, as we shall later see), and become engaged to Elzevira Davidovna Renaissance, who works as a manicurist in her parents' flourishing hair-dressing salon. Prisypkin changes his name to a fashionable Pierre Skripkin (Fiddles), grows sideburns, and buys himself a pair of patent leather shoes. He takes lessons in ballroom dancing and refined manners from Oleg Bayan, a self-styled bard, who also rents rooms. Although he spouts communist rhetoric (as does Bayan, plainly a bourgeois and a wrecker), Prisypkin is quickly becoming a Soviet bourgeois. His wedding feast, celebrated on the premises of the Renaissance hair-dressing salon, is a sumptuous affair in the best tradition of the NEP, a veritable orgy of vulgarity. Bayan entertains the party on the piano, improvises some cute jingles, and toasts the newlyweds, constantly lampooning everything the Revolution had fought for:

What capital steps we are taking forward on our road of family development! Why, when you and I were laying down our lives in the Civil War, and many actually did, could we then have conjectured that these roses would bloom and give us their fragrance even at this early stage of history? As we were still groaning under the yoke of monarchy, could then even our great teachers Marx and Engels have conjecturally dreamed, or even dreamingly conjectured, that we would so soon be united by the bonds of Hymen, obscure yet grandiose Labor and dethroned yet charming Capital? (11:238)

The inevitable happens when the drunken guests start a brawl, during which a blazing stove is turned over. The Renaissance salon goes up in flames, and firemen cannot save a single member of the wedding party. It being winter, the site of the fire soon resembles a skating rink. The firemen conclude part 1 by instructing the audience that vodka and a gasoline stove may be a deadly combination.

The second part is set fifty years later, in 1979. Prisypkin's body, frozen solid, has been discovered and sent to the Institute of Human Resurrection. The resuscitation of so ancient a body requires a vote of the Global Federation, since there is a danger that germs and parasites which infested the population in 1929 might return to life with the human subject, but electronic balloting produces an instantaneous and overwhelmingly affirmative decision. Prisypkin is resurrected over the protests of one laboratory assistant, an elderly woman named Zoya. Resurrected along with him is a bedbug which, back in 1929, had caused Bayan to instruct Prisypkin in a technique of scratching himself unobtrusively, under the cover of an attack of noble jealousy.

Prisypkin immediately discovers that he is a total stranger in the new world: even handshaking has long since been abandoned as an unsanitary habit. There are no horses or even people in the streets, just strange looking automobiles. The one familiar thing in sight is the bedbug, which has crawled from Prisypkin's collar onto the white hospital wall. In despair, Prisypkin tearfully greets the bedbug, then collapses in Zoya's arms.

In the next scene, the worst fears of those opposed to Prisypkin's resurrection have materialized. Prisypkin's guitar strumming and mawkish love songs have infected hundreds of young citizens with a disease called "love," that is, a pathological concentration of normally well distributed sexual energy into a brief period of time. Also, some medical attendants have acquired from him the noxious habit of swilling a fermented beverage called "beer," prepared for him to ease his transition to a useful life, and hundreds of citizens are hospitalized with symptoms of acute poisoning. Many other, younger citizens are going through horrible contortions while locked in tight embrace—Prisypkin has taught them to do the foxtrot. Prisypkin has wrought havoc even upon quadrupeds, by teaching dogs to stand on their hind legs and beg for tidbits. This behavior assumes such proportions that some fear an epidemic of fawning and groveling may spread even among the human population. All these disconcerting developments are, however, forgotten when the exciting news of the discovery of an animal species long considered extinct is announced. The scene ends in the triumphant capture of the bedbug, which will become the pride of the local zoo. In the meantime, scientists labor to raise Prisypkin to a human level, while themselves avoiding infection and preventing him from doing more damage. Zoya concludes the scene by saying: "And fifty years ago I could have died on account of such scum!"

In the final scene, Prisypkin has been caged in the local zoo, whose main attraction he will be, and a large crowd of people, including many foreign correspondents, have gathered to hear the director's edifying inaugural speech. Painstaking research has revealed, he says, that Prisypkin is a specimen of *philistinus vulgaris,* a "terrible humanoid simulator and most amazing parasite," whose life-style strikingly resembles that of the other parasite, *bedbugus normalis.* However, its powers of camouflage and mimicry are far greater: it may attract its unsuspecting hosts by posing as a poetic cricket or a sweet-voiced, romance-warbling bird.

After the director assures the crowd that the creature has been rendered completely harmless, since the noxious fumes it emits are filtered through special ventilators, as is its language, with only perfectly innocuous expressions allowed to penetrate the glass walls of its cage, Prisypkin is allowed to leave his cage to say "something brief, imitating human diction, voice, and language." Here then, in an obvious echo of the mayor's famous declaration in Gogol's *Inspector-General,* Prisypkin addresses the audience: "Citizens! Brothers! My own pals! Friends! Where you all from? How many of you?! When were you all unfrozen? Why am I alone in my cage? Brothers, pals, come join me! Why must I suffer so?! Citizens!" The crowd of 1979, frightened and puzzled, begs the director to desist and Prisypkin is hustled back to his cage, as the director assures the crowd that the creature is suffering from hallucinations.

Like Gogol's *Inspector-General, The Bedbug* is a great play first and foremost because the wealth of its language offers the director and actor virtually unlimited possibilities, and because the main character—the mayor in *The Inspector-General* and Prisypkin in *The Bedbug*—is in each case a symbolic figure permitting many different interpretations. Gogol later regarded his play as an allegory of the human soul, which must eventually answer for its sins and follies, and not before the tractable, but false, inspector of worldly opinion, but before the true inspector of one's conscience. *The Bedbug,* too, is an allegoric presentation of the folly, vulgarity, and heartlessness of humanity. But instead of "conscience," it is fifty years of communism which will transform man and society. The message of Mayakovsky's play—like Gogol's—is ambiguous: perhaps the mayor will trick the "real" inspector too, and Prisypkin only too easily infects the new world with all his old vices.[6]

Mayakovsky's utopia is an intriguing one. Each of its details is anchored in Soviet reality, and each admits a positive as well as a negative interpretation. It is possible that Mayakovsky's antipathy for the Russia of the NEP period was so strong that he saw the inane but sanitized banality of 1979 as a desirable alternative to the dirty, if colorful, vulgarity of 1929, and the smugly bland types of 1979 as an answer to humanity's problems. In other words, an equivalent of Gogol's "Dénouement of *The Inspector-General*" may be included in Mayakovsky's play. But this is only one way to read it.

*The Bathhouse* is less of a play and more of a spectacle than *The Bedbug*, as well as even more obviously an allegory. (The title is allegorical, too: the play will wash away all the dirt in Russia.) What there is of a plot is provided by a time machine, devised—with proper credits to H. G. Wells and Albert Einstein—by the Soviet inventor Chudakov ("Oddball"—all the names in the play are frankly allegoric). The time machine is capable of transporting one into the age of communism (A.D. 2030, to be exact), and vice versa. The invention explodes (figuratively and eventually literally too) in a world that is anything but ready for communism, a Russia populated by totally ineffectual but wholly self-satisfied bureaucrats, careerists, and toadies. *The Bedbug* had dealt with the crude vulgarity of the Soviet petit bourgeois. *The Bathhouse* describes the smug vulgarity of the Soviet elite: party functionaries, newspaper reporters, secretaries, and such. Led by Pobedonosikov (there is a nasty dig even in the name: Konstantin Pobedonostsev was a notoriously reactionary minister under Czar Alexander III), head of the Department of Compromise, these characters try to stop the march of time.

Pobedonosikov, one of whose duties it is to follow the arts and culture, attends a ballet rehearsal and wholeheartedly approves of "imaginary working masses arising symbolically" and "capitalism expiring spectacularly, going into colorful convulsions," but he also insists that scenes which deal disrespectfully with high communist dignitaries such as himself be removed. Midway in the play, a "phosphorescent woman" from the year 2030 bursts onto the scene as a result of a short in Chudakov's time machine. From here on the action is based on a variety of realized time metaphors, the last of which is the train of time which carries its passengers into the communist future. The bureaucrats, careerists, toadies, foreign capitalists, and their stooges are thrown off the train, as Pobedonosikov wails: "I've been run over by Time!"

Meyerhold thought *The Bathhouse* one of the great plays of all time, and Mayakovsky seems to have been genuinely proud of it. The dialogue, to be sure, is racy throughout, except perhaps in the moralizing tirades of the phosphorescent woman, and the famous "March of Time" is a truly rousing poem. The crisp satire has lost none of its cutting edge even in the Soviet Union of today. But then, the train plunging into the future, away from the hopeless banality of the present, takes the audience nowhere in particular. All the play's fireworks do not make the time machine believable. The work has no plot or structure, and leaves a generally chaotic impression. The dialogue is for the most part of the "dialogue of the deaf" kind, that is, there is no dialogue as such. The play's least forgettable character, Mr. Pont Kitsch, a crafty foreign capitalist who would like to buy Chudakov's machine, speaks a transrational futurist language (words that sound Russian but carry no coherent meaning), which his interpreter, Mme Mésalliance, translates into Russian officialese. All this suggests that *The Bathhouse* should be read—and staged—as an absurdist play celebrating the intellectual, administrative, and emotional bankruptcy of Stalin's Russia.

## Mayakovsky on Poetry

Mayakovsky's best poetry of his last period deals with poetry itself, the image of the poet, the poet and society. Apparently these concerns were closer to Mayakovsky's heart than any others, and his personal identity had by then merged with his identity as a poet. Even in the two major poems of 1928 occasioned by Mayakovsky's infatuation with Tatyana Yakovleva we hear the poet more than the lover, which is not the case in the poems devoted to Lilya Brik. In "Conversation with a Tax Collector about Poetry" (1926) and in Mayakovsky's *Exegi monumentum*, "At the Top of My Voice" (1930), the poet regards himself first and foremost as an expert craftsman whose services are of great value to society. Through a series of brilliantly conceived metaphors he explains to the tax collector how difficult the poet's craft is: a verse ending is like an I.O.U., for it requires payment in the form of a rhyme; poetry is like the mining of radium—thousands of tons of verbal ore must be sifted through to obtain a single gram of powerful poetry; and has not the poet huge travel expenses, having perhaps ridden to death a dozen Pegasuses in the last fifteen years? And what about amortization? Does not the poet gradually write himself out? And what about "that most terrible of amortizations, / the amortization / of heart and soul"? (7:124).

Mayakovsky also maintains that the poet's work is useful and important. In "What are You Complaining About?" (1929), he tells Russia's poets and writers:

> Get down
> >       from the sky,
> >               you who dwell in the clouds!
> Take off
> >       the mantle of antiquity!
> With the strongest
> >           of bonds
> >               harness the Muse,
> like a horse,
> >           to the cart of
> >               day-to-day needs.
> >                   (10:143)

In "At the Top of My Voice," Mayakovsky imagines his poetry reaching posterity "as an aqueduct, / built by / the slaves of Rome, / has come down to us." He does not care for poetic immortality:

> I don't give a damn
> >               about any tons of bronze,
> I don't give a damn
> >               about any slimy marble.
> Let's pool our glory—
> >               we're all in the same boat—
> let's agree
> >       that our common monument be
> socialism
> >       built by all of us
> >               in battles.
> >                   (10:284)

At all times he insists that his main poetic virtue is his loyalty to the communist cause: "At the Top of My Voice" ends with the words: "Appearing / before the CCC [Central Committee of the Party] / of the bright years / of future, // over a band / of poetic /

racketeers and crooks, // I shall raise / as my Bolshevik party membership card // all hundred volumes / of my / party books" (10:285).

All this is a signal retreat from the cosmic exuberance of Mayakovsky's personal poetry of earlier years. To be sure, occasional cosmic imagery occurs in Mayakovsky's later poetry, but one senses that his heart is not quite in it anymore. However, in the unfinished draft of a poem four lines of which became a part of Mayakovsky's suicide note, the cosmic imagery recurs strongly:

It is past one o'clock. Must be you've gone to bed.
In the night the Milky Way, like a silvery Oka.[7]
I'm in no hurry and there's no reason for me
to wake you up and disturb you with the lightnings of my cables.
As they say, the incident is closed.
The love boat wrecked by daily life.
You and I are all even and nothing would be gained by listing
mutual hurts, troubles, and insults.
Just look what stillness in the world.
Night has imposed a starry tribute on the sky.
It is in such hours that one rises and speaks to
the ages, history, and the universe.

(10:287)

But how subdued are these lines compared to the boundless energy in the cosmic poetic flights of the early Mayakovsky! And furthermore the imagery is rather conventionally romantic.

"At the Top of My Voice" is perhaps Mayakovsky's finest poem from a technical viewpoint. In it his command of rhythm and sound patterns is at its most virtuosic, and its imagery is wonderfully apt and expressive. Mayakovsky's craftsmanship is the more impressive for being applied to a content which does no credit to the poet's dignity. Mayakovsky's declaration that he had "stepped on the throat of his own songs" to become a political agitator, coupled with the revelation that "he, too, / was sick and tired / of doing propaganda bits," effectively confirms what his detractors had claimed all along, namely, that he had voluntarily become a literary hack. Meanwhile, his assertion that "scribbling / romances, / like the others did, / would have been more profitable / and prettier," is disingenuous, for Mayakovsky gained more worldly fame—and more material rewards too—for his propaganda verse than any poet who was his contemporary. Mandelshtam, Akhmatova, and Pasternak, poets at least as great as Mayakovsky, were living in relative obscurity, eking out a meager income as translators and such, while Mayakovsky was making annual trips abroad, wearing custom-made suits, and riding in his own chauffeur-driven car. A detached analysis of "At the Top of My Voice" will show the poet as a primadonna wallowing in self-pity, but the poem's rhetoric and rhythm are so compelling that they take any audience by storm.

"At the Top of My Voice" is, like Pushkin's "Exegi monumentum" (1836), a summing-up, a statement made by a poet at the end of his career. In each case the author was only thirty-six years of age at the time of writing, and in each case he was dead within a matter of months. In Mayakovsky's case there is nothing uncanny about it all. Mayakovsky had viewed himself from the vantage point of future generations years earlier, in *Man* and in *About That*, for example, and the suicide theme had appeared frequently in his poetry ever since *The Backbone Flute*.

# Chapter Five
# Critical Assessment

## On Versification

Mayakovsky's originality was very pronounced in the form of his verse, and most of all in his versification, which confused critics and scholars for decades. A controversy over the metric structure of Mayakovsky's verse raged for a long time and was ultimately resolved only by exhaustive statistical analysis conducted by scholars with mathematical expertise, such as A. N. Kolmogorov, A. M. Kondratov, and Mikhail Gasparov.

Mayakovsky himself claimed total ignorance of metric theory and said he could not tell an iamb from a trochee. He could, of course, and he also had an unerring rhythmic sense which allowed him not only to duplicate, but also to parody any meter or rhythm known to Russian poetry. Mayakovsky's verse is declamatory, and hence he early formed the habit of printing his verse "stairway fashion," that is, breaking down his lines by moving one space down after each pause:

> Comrade tax collector!
> > Pardon the intrusion.
> Thank you . . .
> > don't bother . . .
> > > I'll stand. . . .
> > > (7:119)

Very often this technique conceals a conventional syllabotonic meter. In 1929 the satirical journal *Krokodil* [Crocodile] printed Mayakovsky's poem "Party Candidates" twice, once in "stairway fashion" and once as regular trochaic tetrameter, asking readers to let the editor know which they liked better.

The formalist scholar Boris Eichenbaum spoke of "melodic" and "rhetorical" types of poets: the former is concerned more with euphonic and rhythmic effects, the latter with expression. Mayakovsky belongs to the latter type. Whenever his verses have a soft lilt or an irresistible driving rhythm, that regularity is invariably symbolic of their content. Mayakovsky uses rhythm and meter as an expressive device, rather than as a rigid form for his poems. This has caused some scholars to speak of Mayakovskian "free verse." Actually, Mayakovsky's poetry exhibits every form, including the extremes of conventional syllabotonic verse and free verse (that is, lines with a random number of syllables and stresses) and a variety of forms between them. Mayakovsky's verses are, however, always rhymed. Very rarely are they stanzaically structured.

Rhymed lines of varying length *(raeshnik)* are known in Russian folk poetry. Pushkin used this form in one of his fairy tales, "The Tale of the Priest and Balda, His Hired Hand," and Mayakovsky employed it frequently, especially in his earlier propaganda poetry, and in much of *150,000,000*. In this type of line Mayakovsky comes closest to prose. But even here a distinct shift away from the rhythm of prose and toward that of verse is possible. Mayakovsky accomplishes this by introducing a significantly higher rate of alliteration, assonance, and inner rhyme than would normally occur in prose discourse, as well as by emphatic stresses and pauses that would not appear in ordinary speech (a device called "accentological estrangement" by Roman Jakobson). Printing a line "stairway fashion" is Mayakovsky's way of indicating such pauses.

More often than not, Mayakovsky's apparent "free verse" is really stress verse, meaning that the number of stresses in a line is a constant (usually two, three, or four), while the number of unstressed syllables varies. In Russian versification, stress verse in which the number of unstressed syllables between stresses alternates between one and two in a random way is called *dol'nik,* and stress verse in which the number of unstressed syllables is unspecified is called *aktsentnyi stikh* ("accentual verse"). Much of Mayakovsky's poetry consists of lines belonging to one of these two types. "Accentual verse" is his proper domain, however: it was called "Mayakovskian verse" at one time, although Mayakovsky was not the first Russian poet to use it.

As for syllabotonic verse, Mayakovsky wrote many purely iambic and trochaic poems and lines. His propaganda jingles are often composed in regular iambic or trochaic lines and stanzas. Often the meter of a given line is closer to a regular syllabotonic pattern than the printed text suggests. For example, a 150-line poem of 1929, "Criticism of Self-Criticism," is printed "stairway fashion," but is written almost entirely in quatrains of trochaic tetrameters with an *a b a b* rhyme scheme. One of the quatrains provides a valuable cue: its last line reads *"chèm /* semnádtstogò razryáda" ("than / the seventeenth grade") instead of a grammatical "chèm / semnádtsatogo razryáda," which would not yield a regular trochaic line. Taking this cue, we can easily remove most of the other "irregularities" through colloquially contracted or slurred pronunciation. That this is fully in order is proved by several instances in which the rhyme demands precisely such a pronunciation (for example, the first quatrain rhymes *kútso* with *sàmokrìtikúetsya,* suggesting a pronunciation *sàmokrìtikútsa* ).

Mayakovsky specialized in what have been called "free iambs" and "free trochees," that is, poems or sections of poems whose basic rhythm is that of a trochaic or iambic line of constant length, but with more or less frequent deviations. Here too, in actual recitation some extra syllables may be eliminated through contraction or slurring, while syncopated weak syllables may be compensated for by suitable pauses. Thus, one can recognize in some of Mayakovsky's best-known poems, though printed "stairway fashion," familiar syllabotonic meters: a trochaic hexameter (with caesura) in "Camp 'Nit Gedajge' "; an iambic pentameter in "At the Top of My Voice"; a trochaic tetrameter in "Idyl" (1928); an iambic tetrameter in "An Extraordinary Adventure"; and even an alexandrine in "Get Ready! Stand! Build!" ("Gotov'sya! Stoy! Stroy!" 1928).

Nikolay Nekrasov (1821–78) was the first Russian poet consistently to use ternary meters (dactyls, anapests, and amphibrachs) in longer poems. Nekrasov must have appealed to Mayakovsky not only as an innovator, but also as a civic poet with revolutionary leanings. Mayakovsky's ternary meters, like his binary meters, appear in a "free" version, and are especially prominent in Mayakovsky's longer poems and verse epics, such as *Man* and *About That.* It may be that the meter of Mayakovsky's "Harvest March" (1929), one of his few poems devoted to the peasantry, was chosen directly under Nekrasov's influence: it is composed in the basic (iambic) meter of Nekrasov's principal work *Who Has a Good Life in Russia?*

Mayakovsky is a great master of the ditty *(chastushka),* usually a quatrain of rhymed trochaic tetrameters with a "punch line." He uses the form most effectively in his didactic and propaganda verse.

Finally, Mayakovsky was a virtuoso of parody who could imitate any meter or rhythm: that of a romance; of "Pushkinian" iambs (in "Anniversary Poem" or in the parody of *Eugene Onegin* in the fourth episode of *Good!*); of Lermontovian trochaic pentameter; or of Aleksey Tolstoy's ballad of the 1840s (in amphibrachs) "Vasily Shibanov" (in "Ballad about the Bureaucrat and the Worker-Correspondent," 1928). Naturally, the section of *About That* entitled "The Ballad of Reading Gaol" starts out with Oscar Wilde's meter—but only as a tease, since Mayakovsky quickly moves on to other rhythms.

Mayakovsky's longer poems are remarkable for the variety and elasticity of their rhythmic composition. Not only does he constantly shift from stress meters (or free verse) to syllabotonic meters and back, he also uses different syllabotonic and accentual meters (or *dol'niki*) in lines of different length. *About That* is particularly interesting in this regard, as is "Letter to Comrade Kostrov from Paris, on the Nature of Love." In the latter, amphibrachs, trochaic tetrameters, and trochaic trimeters appear in a dazzling variety of free rhythms; each shift of meter coincides with a shift of mood.

## On Rhyme

Mayakovsky considered rhyme an indispensable part of his verse. "Why?" he asked. "Because without rhyme the verse will fall to pieces. Rhyme returns you to the preceding line, forces you to remember it, holds together all the lines that form a single thought" ("How to Make Verses" [12:105]).

This view is shared by students of Mayakovsky's verse. One of them, Mikhail Shtokmar, thought it more important than stress, so that Mayakovsky's verse should be called "rhymed verse." This is a misconception, for rhyme is to a large extent an integral part of the rhythmic structure of Mayakovsky's verse. Line boundaries are marked by rhyme, while inner rhyme, exceedingly common in Mayakovsky, creates a pause ("caesura") within a line. Rhyme has other functions as well: often rhyming words, or groups of words, form a meaningful juxtaposition, either serious or funny. Then too, Mayakovsky frequently plays with the suspense which the anticipation of a rhyme may produce. He dramatizes this device in the prologue to *About That* by printing an ellipsis instead of its last word, which must rhyme with *lbov* ("foreheads"), and so must be *lyubov'* ("love"), the theme of the poem.

Rhyme may be used as a device to string the narrative together: this is spectacularly the case in *Good!*, where a series of epiphoric rhymes (the last word of a line rhyming with the first word of the following line) introduces the description of revolutionary unrest gripping the country. Clearly these rhymes symbolize the chain reaction described in this second episode of the poem.

Ingenious, punning, or otherwise witty rhymes are entertaining *per se*.[1] Mayakovsky makes a point of finding rhymes for even the most outlandish—from a Russian viewpoint—foreign names, such as da Vinci, Lloyd George, Churchill, and MacDonald.

Mayakovsky's rhymes differ significantly from those of nineteenth-century poets. The latter created rhyme by repetition of the last stressed vowel of a line and the vowels and consonants following it, for example, kup*éts:* ot*éts;* m*óre:* g*óre*. In Mayakovsky's poetry the rhyme shifts to the left: the correspondence to the right of the last stress is only approximate (sometimes nonexistent), while a correspondence to the left of it is actively pursued, for example, *zven*ó: *zv*on*ók*; sir*énnye r*ó*koty*: vr*émya-d*ó*ktor* (*About That*). The latter pair is a closer rhyme than the transcription suggests, since *rókoty* may be slurred into *rókty*. The extension of the rhyme to the left is not obligatory. Thus, in the example just given, the rhyme *zven*ó: *zvon*ó*k* is supported even further to the left, while the rhyme with which it alternates has no such support. The whole quatrain reads:

> Ne m*ó*lknet v s*é*rdtse b*ó*l' *nik*ák,
> kuy*ó*t k *zven*ú *zven*ó.
> Vot t*á*k,
>      ub*í*v, Rask*ó*l'*nik*ov
> khod*í*l *zvon*ít' *zvon*ók.

> The pain just won't stop in my heart,
> forging link to link.
> Must be that's how,
>           Raskolnikov
> went to ring the bell, after the murder.
>                (4:167)

Of course Mayakovsky also uses a large number of rhymes that are correct even by nineteenth-century standards. The share of genuine trick rhymes is not very large, but Mayakovsky occasionally treats his audience to rhyming fireworks. There are, for example, compound rhymes:

> Lét do *stá*
>           *rastí*
> nám
>      bez *stárosti.*
> Gód ot góda
>           *rasti*
> náshey bódr*osti.*
> Sláv'te,
>      *mólo*t i *stí*kh,
> zémlyu *mólo*do*sti.*

> To a hundred years
>                     grow
> we shall
>           without aging.
> Year after year
>                shall grow
> our energy.
> Praise,
>      hammer and verse,
>                          our land of youth.
>                          (*Good!* 1927 [8:328])

This is the conclusion of one of Mayakovsky's major political poems. He must have cherished these fanciful rhymes to put them in such an exposed position.

So-called "summary" rhyme is believed to be Mayakovsky's original invention. Here is an example from a poem composed for the windows of ROSTA in 1920:

> Pány krásnym tkút *petlyú,*
> nám mogílu *róyu*t.
> Ssýp' v mogílu étu *tlyú*
> vméste s *Petlyuróyu!*

> The Polish *Pans* are spinning us a noose,
> digging our grave.
> Flick those mites into their grave,
> together with Petlyura!
>                          (3:89)

Here *petlyu* ("noose") + *royut* ("dig") = *Petlyuroyu* ("Petlyura" was a Ukrainian nationalist leader and a bitter enemy of the Bolsheviks). Some of Mayakovsky's most virtuosic rhymes may be found in his propaganda ditties, commercial jingles, and poster legends. This example is taken from a series of posters presenting the "heroes" and "enemies" of the Revolution (1918). It has to do with one of the enemies, the merchant *(kupets):*

> Ékh, poydú, moí *ottsý,*
> s górya *nalizát'sya ya.*
> Svéta blízyatsya k*ontsý—*
> *nàtsionalizátsiya.*

> Eh, my dear ones, I'll go
> and get plastered to drown my sorrow.
> The end of the world is near—
> nationalization.
> (2:91)

Other games Mayakovsky plays with end rhyme are whimsical rather than brilliant. In a poem composed on the occasion of an international congress of Young Communists—"Greetings, K.I.M.!" (1928)—every second line either rhymes with KIM, or ends in KIM, all of which is rather labored. In a long poem (over fifty lines), "A Note to China" (1929), every rhyme responds to some case form of *Kitay,* "China." All six Russian cases are represented, some several times. In another lengthy poem, "The Leninists" (1930), Mayakovsky plays the same game with Lenin's patronymic, Ilich. In these efforts Mayakovsky wittingly or unwittingly follows amazingly closely, in content as well as form, the traditions of eighteenth-century ceremonial poetry.

Mayakovsky, who consistently broke through the conventional constraints of poetic form, assiduously cultivated the free forms of sound patterning, such as alliteration, assonance, and inner rhyme. In this area he stayed with his futurist predilections to the end.

Mayakovsky is a virtuoso at using sound patterns symbolically. In *About That,* for instance, sound symbolism appears in massive doses. Thus, the lapping of the imaginary water which fills the poet's flat is described in several lines in which the word *voda* (pronounced *vadá*) seems to be everywhere:

Chórt*ova* *vá*nna!
         V*odá* za *divá*nom.
P*od* stolóm,
           za shká*fo*m *vodá.*
S *divá*na,
           sd*ví*nut *vodý* zad*evá*n'em,
*v o*knó proplýl chem*odá*n.

Damned water!
           Water behind the sofa.
Under the table,
           behind the wardrobe.
Pushed from the sofa
           by the water,
my suitcase swims out the window.
                                    (4:148)

Sound effects of this type may also render the uproar of a drunken party, a dance rhythm, the monotonous lilt of a ballad recital, and so on. In "At the Top of My Voice," another poem saturated with sound patterning, Mayakovsky sneers at the folksy young romantic poets of his age, by first quoting a popular romance, and then grotesquely realizing its central metaphor ("poetry is a flower garden, to be gently watered"), all of it accompanied by a lot of sing-song sound repetition, and finally topping it all with an amazing pun involving the names of two of his victims: "Kudrevátye Mitreýki, mudrevátye Kudreýki" ("Curly Mitreykos, abstruse Kudreykos"). These two poets—Konstantin Mitreykin and Anatoly Kudreyko—actually existed, but their only claim to fame was to be to have figured in this pun. *Kudrevatyi* ("curly") is used figuratively to mean "askew, wayward, crooked," yet curly hair is the proverbial attribute of the young lover in Russian popular romances. *Mudrevatyi* is likewise ambiguous, as it means "shrewd, clever," but also "abstruse, puzzling, hard to figure out."

One of the most magnificent passages in all of Mayakovsky is his dream of a conquest of time in "Camp 'Nit Gedajge.'" (In the lines preceding those quoted here, the poet dreams of the advantages if time could weave cloth instead of hours:)

     V*p*réch' by éto
              *v*rémya
                 *v pri*vodnóy by *ré*men',—

*spústyat*
  *s* kholos*tógo—*
          i *ch*eshí i *sýp'!*
*Ch*tóby
    ne *ch*asý pokázyvali *vrém*ya,
  a *ch*tob *vrém*ya
          *chést*no
            dvígalo *ch*asý.

  Oh, to hitch up
            time
              to a driving belt,
    take it
        out of neutral,
              let it go full swing.
  So that
      no clock will tell time,
    but time will
          honestly
              move clocks.

                    (7:89)

Here the driving rhythm of a trochaic hexameter (with a caesura after the third foot) combines with a wealth of inner rhyme, assonance, and alliteration to suggest the rapid and regular movement of an efficient time machine.

Mayakovsky's active search for sound patterns is not always so well motivated. Often enough it is simply an outpouring of virtuoso exuberance. Mayakovsky is an inexhaustible producer of puns, by no means all of which are brilliant, or even good. He also has an acute sense of what his friend Roman Jakobson would later call "the poetry of grammar," that is, manipulating grammatical forms and emphasizing them for dramatic effect. For example, the refrain of a lengthy poem of 1924, "The Young Communist," is: "Lenin / lived, // Lenin / lives, // Lenin / will live" (6:34–38). The refrain rhymes with the preceding lines, and not only phonetically, but even semantically: the concept of a past that is still present and extends into the future dominates the poem throughout. A similar pattern occurs in a eulogy to a Soviet diplomat assassinated by a political opponent in Switzerland, "Vorovsky" (1923). Still, the "poetry of grammar" is not always truly poetic. In "Evpatoriya" (1928), a 41-line poem, Mayakovsky uses ten different forms of

Evpatoriya, a city in the Crimea—a rather annoying exercise in declension. But in some other instances, he brings forward a grammatical category—such as tense, aspect, or number—creatively and effectively.

Mayakovsky's imagery displays the same breadth as his versification and sound patterning. One area in which he took little interest is nature imagery—he left the birch groves and corn flowers to Esenin. The great range of Mayakovsky's imagery is attributable not only to his extraordinary receptiveness, mobility, and curiosity, but also to the fact that he worked in an exceptionally wide spectrum of poetic genres.

## Mayakovsky as Classicist

None among Mayakovsky's contemporaries—if we limit ourselves to poets of his caliber—was a consistent writer of panegyric, solemn, celebratory, and occasional odes, as he was. Hence one finds in Mayakovsky's poetic arsenal certain archaic vocabulary and imagery which link him directly to eighteenth-century classicism. These archaic images are mixed with modern prosaisms, but this was also true—*mutatis mutandis*—of Gavriil Derzhavin, Russia's greatest poet of the eighteenth century. An example from Mayakovsky's "Comintern" (1923) will illustrate this:

Gazing
          into the approaching storm,
                                        into approaching thunder clouds,
          thundering ahead through waves of time,
                                        through waves of space,
          the rudder
                    of stormy days
                              in mighty grip,
          along the Moscow river
                              sails
                    the dreadnought of
                                        the Comintern.
                                                    (5:73)

Every word in these lines could have been taken from a solemn patriotic ode of the eighteenth century except for the phrase "the dreadnought of the Comintern." The image of the ship of state, guided through stormy seas by a trusted helmsman's mighty hand, is as old as Western poetry: we find it in Alcaeus, who flourished in the seventh century B.C. Incidentally, the lines quoted here are also saturated with alliteration and are exceedingly well suited for declamation. Poetically, this piece—and many others like it celebrating the October Revolution, Red Army Day, Lenin and other communist heroes, the physical fitness of Soviet athletes, the anniversary of the Paris Commune, the Komsomol, the Soviet police, and other such things—all these pieces are as a rule woefully pedestrian. But they also contain a tremendous amount of imagery testifying to the breadth of Mayakovsky's imagination.

Another genre that links Mayakovsky directly to classicism is the satirical character sketch in the manner of La Bruyère: "The Pillar of Society," "The Coward," "The Gossip," "The Hypocrite," "The Lickspittle" (all 1928), and others. Here Mayakovsky is in his element as he piles one graphic image upon another in describing, for example, the lickspittle: "Licks his foot, / and licks his hands, // licks his belt, / and licks below it, // like a puppy / licks a bitch, / / like a kitten / licks a cat" (9:360). Yet another neoclassical genre represented in Mayakovsky is the fable, sometimes in pure form (for example, "Verses on Different Tastes," 1928), and sometimes as an element of other genres, as in Mayakovsky's pieces for children.

A number of Mayakovsky's postrevolutionary poems were versified editorials covering the whole range of daily news, from General Umberto Nobile's illfated polar expedition ("A Cross and Champagne," "Strange . . . but True," both 1928) to a campaign to avert the closing of the Moscow Children's Theater ("The Childrens Theater, Evicted from its Home by Comrade Satirists," 1928). As a rule, Mayakovsky's versified editorials may be easily linked to prose editorials or news items appearing in the same paper or journal, or one of approximately the same time. For example, on the same page of *Pravda* for 21 July 1928 we find an editorial by a staff writer entitled "Let's Launch the Battle for Cheap, High Quality, and Comfortable Housing!", and Mayakovsky's poem, "Comrades, Shall we ever See Good Housing? Comrades, Build Well and Cheap!" Both pieces maintain that the flow of money into private housing co-ops should be discouraged and the government entrusted with the resolution of the housing crisis.

It is quite in accord with Mayakovsky's aesthetics that his muse should address herself to minor topics of mundane interest: he would versify on absolutely any topic. He will address an ode to "Comrade Typist" (1927) extolling the virtues of that much maligned toiler; he will bemoan the poet's futile search throughout Moscow for a decent pair of socks to fit his feet ("In Search of Socks," 1928)— in short, Mayakovsky wrote versified feuilletons dealing with the prose of everyday life, and did as conscientious a job of it as of all his other work. The journalistic genre, then, in conjunction with his didactic, edifying, and commercial verses, accounts for a large portion of Mayakovsky's imagery and vocabulary. And all of that, once conquered by verse, spills over into those of Mayakovsky's poems which few will deny the status of "art." Thus Mayakovsky vastly expanded the range of poetic expression, rather as Pushkin had in his day. He was not alone in this, of course. Pasternak's poetry of everyday life, Nikolay Zabolotsky's magnificent genre scenes of Soviet city life in Pushkinian verse, the civic poetry of Mayakovsky's friend Nikolay Aseev, all moved in the same direction. In fact, only Mayakovsky's ever present didacticism prevented his "Walks through Streets and Alleys" (there is a cycle by that title, 1926) from creating a truly vivid picture of life in the Soviet Union under the NEP. Still, he wrote some genre pieces which approach, though never quite equal, the best of Zabolotsky, for example, "Herzen House" (1928), a graphic description of a sleazy night spot located in the basement of Alexander Herzen's former Moscow home, with several literary organizations housed on the top floors.

Like his classicist predecessors, Mayakovsky wrote a great deal of versified literary criticism and polemics. Besides great poems, such as "To Sergey Esenin" or "Conversation with a Tax-Collector about Poetry," he wrote many minor pieces, such as "Marxism is a Weapon, a Method of Firearm Quality—so Use this Method Knowledgeably!" (1926), "Fourfold Hackwork" (1926, "fourfold" means Gosizdat, criticism, reader, and writer), and "To Workers in the Field of Verse and Prose, Who will Spend this Summer on a Collective Farm" (1928). Mayakovsky even composed at least one versified theater review: "Let's have Some Rotten Eggs! Review No. 1" (1928). In this case Mayakovsky had made a public show of disapproval (whistling as loudly as he could, which was very loudly) during a performance of Vsevolod Pushmin's play *A Room to Pass Through*. He disapproved of the play's eroticism, which he found vulgar, and gave a detailed account of it in a 110-line poem.

Mayakovsky, a poet of great histrionic talent and a master of parody, could produce lines in any style or manner he wished. This also broadened the range of his imagery, which came to include images and phrases from the popular ditty, from the sentimental romance (for example, "Marusya Poisoned Herself," 1927, a ballad in iambics and entirely in the manner of "urban folklore"), from cabaret verse, and even from proletarian verse *à la* Vasily Kazin: "And in the palaces / a different life: // When you've had your fill / of fun by the water, // go, worker, / and lie down // in a Grand-Ducal / bed. // The mountains blaze / like furnaces, // the sea is blue / like a worker's coveralls, // as a speedy repair job / of people proceeds // in that huge / Crimean smithy." ("The Crimea," 1927 [8:145])

Despite his professed hostility to all "literature," and especially that of the past, Mayakovsky frequently incorporated allusions to the works and images of Russian and foreign authors in his poetry. Pushkin, Lermontov, Gogol, Nekrasov, Tolstoy, Dostoevsky, Blok, Esenin, Goethe, Hugo, Maupassant, Wilde, Whitman, Longfellow, and many other major as well as minor authors enrich Mayakovsky's verse by their presence.

Naturally Mayakovsky uses the great art and poetry of the past strictly as material for his own. His "Anniversary Poem" (1924, occasioned by the 125th anniversary of Pushkin's birth) may serve as an example. Here Mayakovsky brazenly jumps across the barrier of time to hustle Pushkin off his pedestal and home to his own flat for a drink and a friendly chat. Of course the host does all the talking, prattling away in a tone of condescending light banter, and quoting—or rather misquoting—Pushkin all along. He regrets that Pushkin is no longer around: he would have made a good editorial assistant on the staff of Mayakovsky's own *Lef,* one who would have learned quickly, one whom one could have trusted even with the composition of all-important propaganda ditties. He suggests that soon enough the two of them will be almost neighbors in the encyclopedia, separated only by Nekrasov, after such small fry as Semyon Nadson are dispensed with (he ought to be filed away under *SHCH,* one of the last letters of the cyrillic alphabet). Mayakovsky admires Pushkin's craftsmanship. Also, along with the official party line, he is willing to admit that Pushkin was "for his times, a progressive." But he also declines to accord him any respect on the grounds that he is a national symbol, or that he was a poet inspired by something transcending ordinary human experience.

We have noted Mayakovsky's frequent use of religious imagery in several of his major poems *(The Cloud in Trousers, The Backbone Flute, Man)*. Religious imagery and biblical and liturgical language are used throughout Mayakovsky's works, but in a spirit of blasphemy or cold sarcasm. For example, a versified political editorial of 1923 condemning the signing of the Treaty of Versailles is entitled: "Peace on Earth and Good Will toward Men." And yet the frankly and straightforwardly sublime is by no means alien to Mayakovsky's work, and the presence of this aesthetic category aligns; him with classicism once again. His ever present cosmic imagery occasionally reaches the heights as well as the mood of a Mikhail Lomonosov, the great eighteenth-century ode writer:

> I can see,
>         see clearly, down to details.
> Air to air,
>         like stone to stone,
> unassailable to putrefaction and to crumbling,
> bursting into brilliance,
>         towering through the ages,
> the workshop of human resurrection.
> *(About That* [4:181])

Mayakovsky is capable of speaking in the same solemn and lofty sense even of more ordinary human achievement: "We walk on / through the barking of revolvers, // so that, / dying, / we shall become incarnate // in steamers, / lines of verse, / and other long-lived things" ("To Comrade Nette," 1926 [7:164]). Comrade Nette was a Soviet diplomatic courier who died in an exchange of gunfire while defending the mail entrusted to him; subsequently a Soviet steamer was named after him.

## Poet of the Artful Conceit

Mayakovsky is among the most inventive masters in all of Russian poetry of the artful conceit (which smacks of the baroque and of the seventeenth century!). Soviet critics, by and large, have tended to reject the notion that Mayakovsky indulged in verbal play the way

Gogol did in his prose. But it is fairly obvious that in many instances
Mayakovsky's poetic phrase is generated by the power of verbal or
visual association, rather than by the logic of a preconceived idea.
In a way, Mayakovsky's poems are propelled by two forces: one of
emotional energy or rational purpose, and one of an inexhaustible,
often metaphysical, imagination. Mayakovsky put it very well in
*The Backbone Flute:* "I strung out my soul across an abyss, like a
cable, // juggling words, I am swaying over it" (1:206). Moreover,
the artful conceit is by no means limited to Mayakovsky's "personal"
poetry: if anything, his revolutionary and propaganda verses contain
even more of them. A few examples will suffice:

In "The Fifth Internationale" (1922), the Red Star of the U.S.S.R.
is imagined as conquering the world by flooding it with its Red:

> Sweeping away the traces of Norway's frontiers,
> in the North
> the red storm tears along.
> Here
> a second ray burns through the ice,
> coloring the snow crimson all the way to the North Pole.

Or, from the same poem:

> With headlights by Marx and Company
> the automobile of dialectics tore into the years,
> as the future dispersed their darkness.
> (4:131)

The considerable energy of "Camp 'Nit Gedajge,' " certainly a
poem with a revolutionary message, is generated largely by conceits
based on the pathetic fallacy. It begins with a rhetorical question:
might it not be a good idea "to make that rascal, Night, quit
emitting so many starry stings from her jaws." After a series of
similar images, all magnificent, the poem concludes with the song
of the young American communists at Camp Nit Gedajge which
envisions the Hudson flowing into the Moscow River (7:91).
Mayakovsky's imagery often veered toward the hyperbolic, the
grotesque, and the violent, even before the war and the Revolution
gave him ample reason to see the world as grotesque and violent.
Some of Mayakovsky's most violent imagery, involving various horrible forms of execution, occurs in *The Backbone Flute,* a love poem.

Some of the imagery in another love poem, *About That,* where the poet's persona is literally shot to pieces in the end, is quite as gory as the most cruel scenes in *War and the World,* which depicts the horrors of war.

By and large, Mayakovsky's violent images are not really terrible. His grotesque visions of death and destruction are most often those of a satirical cartoonist. Their violence is that of realized metaphor, not of immediate experience. The bayonets which triumphant communist soldiers ram into the fat bellies of cigar-chomping capitalists in his cartoons are metaphoric, not real, and the same is true of most of his poetic images. When the poet expresses his anger at the murder of the Soviet diplomat Vatslav Vorovsky in Lausanne in 1923, he says: "Today / roll / your anger / into a huge / explosive ball" ("Vorovsky," 1923). That image could be easily converted into a cartoon. And in general Mayakovsky liked the image of a bomb. When he describes a Western customs officer who has just been handed Mayakovsky's Soviet passport, he sees the scene thus:

> He takes it
>                 like a bomb,
>                               he takes it
>                                             like a hedgehog,
>             like a double-edged
>                       razor,
>             he takes it
>                 like a snake
>                             two meters long,
>             rattling its 20 fangs.
>                 (10:70)

This example is in many ways characteristic of Mayakovsky's style. The bomb alone would have conveyed the idea, but Mayakovsky goes on to more picturesque similes, all of which represent a merely verbal reality. Rattlesnakes do not rattle with their fangs, and nobody in his right mind picks up a hedgehog, much less a rattlesnake. In a word, Mayakovsky is carried away by images as ends-in-themselves.

In one of his nastier anticapitalist pieces, "The Wrecker" (1928), Mayakovsky supports a hate campaign against Russian engineers who have allegedly become hired agents of capitalism: "Stealthily / he goes / to sabotage the ventilator, // so that coalminers / would howl / choking in their mine-shafts, // like locked up / calves low / in a fire" (9:160). The image is indeed graphic, but a man gasping for air will hardly howl and it is doubtful that Soviet miners appreciated being likened to calves. Mayakovsky is again carried away by a Homeric simile.

Considering the extraordinary richness of Mayakovsky's imagery, metaphoric as well as nonmetaphoric, it is difficult to delineate any categories or groups of images as characteristic of his poetic style. Lawrence L. Stahlberger has established a pattern of archetypal images—such as "bondage," "eternal recurrence," and "cosmic alienation"—in Mayakovsky's poetry.[2] Certainly these motifs appear prominently in some of Mayakovsky's poems (*The Cloud in Trousers, The Backbone Flute, Man, About That*), but not consistently enough to be considered an integral part of Mayakovsky's *Gestalt* as a poet. Stahlberger sees as a characteristic trait of Mayakovsky's poetry a tendency to present the poet's persona as a martyr, a dandy, or a clown and often all of these together. There is much to be said for this: certainly this trait is intimately linked with Mayakovsky's declamatory style, and he assumed all three roles in life as well. But then, these roles, though perhaps not this particular combination of them, are found in many other poets. Esenin, a very different poet in almost every way, assumed quite similar roles.

If one asks, with Gaston Bachelard, whether one of the four elements predominates in Mayakovsky's poetry, one might answer that he is, if anything, an aquarius. In several of his major works (*Mystery-Bouffe, 150,000,000, About That, Good!* "Revolution: A Poetic Chronicle," "Our March") the image of a deluge is prominent. But this is most likely a repetition of a particular conceit, rather than the spontaneous surrender to the element which we find in Pasternak, for example. Mayakovsky's cosmic point of view, and his frequent trips into outer space appear in the work of many other poets of the revolutionary period, including Pasternak. But in Mayakovsky this trait appears even before the Revolution, in *The Backbone Flute* and *Man*, for example. It also fits in with his cosmic alienation, and seems to be an organic trait of his creative personality. It also appears to square with Mayakovsky's perception of time, as I shall try to show below.

Mayakovsky's verbal range is just as wide as the range of his imagery. He obliterates the boundary between poetic language and the language of prose, which exists even in Russian symbolism. The

whole lexicon of the Russian language, from pompous archaisms
and biblical language to technical jargon and the vilest slang, enters
the crucible of Mayakovsky's poetry. Sometimes Mayakovsky utilizes
the social connotation of a word for purposes of irony, pathos,
mockery, solemnity, etc.; sometimes he will ignore it. Georgy Vinokur, in his book *Mayakovskii—novator yazyka* [Mayakovsky as an
Innovator of Language, 1943], suggested that Mayakovsky was pur-
suing a "de-aesthetization" of language which, coincidentally, en-
tailed the destruction of every form of stylized language. This is
correct only in a general way. It is true that Mayakovsky uses bookish
words in poems addressed to the proletariat, and crude vulgarisms
(replaced by ellipses in the Academy edition) in a poem otherwise
very close to the genre of the ode ("At the Top of My Voice"), and
that poems such as *Vladimir Ilich Lenin* and *Good!* are linguistically
and stylistically a hodge-podge. On the other hand, Mayakovsky
can use his lexicon quite discriminatingly when he wishes to convey
a certain impression. He laces his American poems with ample
Anglicisms or outright English words. He works analogously in his
Parisian cycle, and when he wants to present a young poet, pre-
sumably an exponent of the "Parisian note," he lets him say:

> I have a liaison with the Muses.
> My style
>                   has breeding, like a greyhound,
>     *ce qu'on appelle*
>               *la poésie.*
>               (God's Birdie," 1929 [10:112])

In "Kazan" (1928), Mayakovsky actually tries to give his text a
Tartar flavor (Kazan is the capital of the Tartar Autonomous Republic) by introducing vocabulary and syntax which seem "Tartar"
to a Russian. Mayakovsky, a master of social stylization, deftly
captures the traits identifying a person as a proletarian, NEP-man,
bureaucrat, or intellectual, and not only in his plays, but in many
of his poems as well. Finally, Mayakovsky is a superb parodist, with
an unerring ear for the peculiarities of "the other voice."

All in all, Mayakovsky's verbal usage is rich and varied, rather
than "different," as Khlebnikov's is. Mayakovsky's numerous neologisms (the subject of a book-length monograph)[3] are often ingenious and sometimes colorful, but they remain within the confines

of the rules of Russian derivation. Aristophanean compounds such as *verblyudokorabledrakonii* ("camelshipdraconian," from "The Fifth Internationale"); emotionally charged adjectives such as *molotkastyi, serpastyi* ("sporting a hammer and sickle," from "Verses on My Soviet Passport"); abstract nouns derived from concrete nouns, for example, *slonovost'* ("elephantine thickskinnedness," from *slon,* "elephant"); all these and many other word formations are qualitatively well within the limits of normal creative speech. It is the sheer quantity of Mayakovsky's output which is so impressive.

## The Reconciliation of Contradictions

In assessing Mayakovsky's poetic personality as a whole, one is initially struck by a basic and pervasive contradiction. The most egocentric and self-assertive of Russian poets, Mayakovsky was also the bard of a collectivist society and of the Soviet ideal of man, which is profoundly anti-individualist. But this contradiction may be only apparent. Mayakovsky, though egocentric, reveals little of what must have been his inner life. He functions rather as a persona, or "image," or even as an allegory, instead of an individual. His self, assertive though it is, does not resemble the conscience of a religious person, the intense self-consciousness of the existentialist hero, or the persona of psychological fiction. It is an "outer-directed" self of the sort well described in Trotsky's *bon mot:* "In order to uplift man, he raises him to the level of Mayakovsky." Trotsky's irony was justified. Mayakovsky was a genuine lover of Mayakovskian man, but most intolerant of un-Mayakovskian men.

Mayakovsky's titanism, a striking trait of his prerevolutionary poetry, fuses with the revolutionary titanism of the Soviet period. As early as "The Fifth Internationale" (1922), Mayakovsky perceives himself as "a hero / Svyatogor of epics of the future" (4:121). (Svyatogor ["Holy Mountain"] is a mythic giant of the Russian folk epic.) The poem continues:

> So that the poet may outgrow the boundaries of ages,
> so that the poet
>             may lead the army of humanity,
> together with the universe, absorb the juices
> of the earth, your feet grown into it with their roots.
>                                         (4:121)

This allusion to the titan Antaeus of Greek mythology was a cliché of communist rhetoric (Stalin actually recounted the story of Antaeus in one of his speeches). Mayakovsky has the mythical strength of the masses ( = the earth) flow not only into the veins of their leader (Lenin), but also those of the people's poet. Mayakovsky's titanism, which appears in a variety of images throughout his poetry, thus acquires a certain legitimacy. As Johannes R. Becher has put it, Mayakovsky's works "celebrate the birth of a new man, of 'man who has exalted himself to rule over Nature, to free himself and those around him from cruel Necessity' (Goethe)."[4]

Mayakovsky's aggressively antireligious attitude likewise has two sides. In his prerevolutionary poetry, and so still in *About That,* his blasphemy is that of romantic Prometheanism, deriving from a personal struggle with God *(bogoborchestvo).* The poet's persona appears as a rebel and usurper of God's power, rather than as one who simply declares God a superstition of the uneducated. This attitude is also borne out by the poet's frequent identification of himself with Christ, again as in *About That:*

> Upon the bridge of years,
> > > exposed to contempt,
> > > > > to derision,
> ordained redeemer of earthly love,
> I must stand,
> > > I stand for all.
> > > > (4:172)

In his poetry of the Soviet period Mayakovsky appears mostly in the role of communist agitator, one of whose many tasks it is to eradicate religion. God and Christ now become mere objects of mockery.

Mayakovsky's rebellion against God has as its direct corollary a rebellion against nature, which again has two sides. Mayakovsky's futurist *Sturm und Drang* leads to an arbitrary, sometimes chaotic deformation of nature, for no other purpose than to assert the artist's self-will and creative freedom. Later this urge for creative freedom is channeled into the revolutionary ideal of "remaking the world" according to a preconceived idea, Leninist socialism leading to an industrial communist society. The constructivist poetics of *Lef* found a parallel in the planned economy and organized social life of Stalin's Russia:

                        I am ready
                                every day
                                        to repeat a hundred times:
                        Beauty
                                is one-hundred-percent usefulness,
                        comfortable clothes
                                        and spacious living quarters.
                                                                (8:38)

The quote is from "Let's have a Beautiful Life" (1927).

Thus, in a variety of ways, Mayakovsky's art has two sides: one spontaneous and aesthetically motivated, the other disciplined and in the service of the Soviet regime. This is true even of his revolutionary poetry. The relationship between the Revolution and left art was a complex one. At one point it seemed that their paths might merge. But then left art entered its death throes while Mayakovsky was still alive. The Revolution was continuing, though, as Stalin hammered out a wholly new society which turned its back on the avant-garde, even though Mayakovsky was declared by Stalin himself to have been "the best and most talented poet of our Soviet epoch." The constructivist art of *New Lef,* to whose program Mayakovsky heartily subscribed, would have served Stalin's objectives loyally and well. Yet it was abandoned in every art form, including even architecture, abandoned largely for so-called "socialist realism," which was actually a version of nineteenth-century naturalism with a tendency prescribed by the various exigencies of the Soviet government.

Although Soviet critics would like to deny it, there is a rift between Mayakovsky's more personal moods and the attitude of the poet's persona in his civic poetry. The latter is basically optimistic, despite the criticism of the Soviet system found in the civic poetry. But whenever Mayakovsky speaks for himself, his prevailing mood is one of pessimism; moreover, a pessimism born of frustration, boredom, and resignation. *About That* contains these lines:

                        But what about me?
                In my childhood, maybe,
                                        at the very bottom
                I'll find ten
                                bearable days.
                                (4:180)

The suicide theme is ever present in Mayakovsky's personal poetry. The Revolution must have given some meaning to his life, but disillusionment soon cast its shadow even over his political poems. The message of "To Sergey Esenin" is really that there is little to cheer about in life. Mayakovsky's exhortations to young communists who are cruelly disappointed by the good life of the NEP-men and the bleak life of devoted communists have a ring of resignation ("What Did We Fight for?" 1927). What is even worse, at moments Mayakovsky doubted even the value of his own poetry:

> In our country of Soviets,
>                         one can live
> well enough,
>                   and work together well.
> Except for the fact
>                   that there are no poets
>                                       here, I'm sorry to say—
> However, maybe
>                   none are needed, either.
>                   ("Anniversary Poem," 1924 [6:55])

This statement contrasts markedly with Mayakovsky's stubborn defense of the poet's position in the forefront of progress. (This quite aside from the fact that Mayakovsky claims there "are no poets" in Russia at a time when Pasternak, Akhmatova, Mandelshtam, and Esenin, to name but a few, were at the height of their powers.) Still, in the same poem Mayakovsky also said: "For me, / and for you too, / eternity is in store" (6:47): he is addressing Pushkin, to a Russian the immortal poet *par excellence*. In "At the Top of My Voice," written five years later, Mayakovsky conceives of his immortality differently: it will not be the immortality of his name and oeuvre, but the anonymous immortality of the honest worker for a better life. In a sense, then, Mayakovsky finds even here a way to make Mayakovsky the mouthpiece of the Soviet regime a logical continuation of Mayakovsky the futurist genius.

## Mayakovsky and Time

Along with several Soviet and Western critics, I believe that Mayakovsky's perception of time is the most revealing feature of his imagination. Mayakovsky was one of the most time-conscious among many such poets of his age. His time philosophy was pointed and consistent, his time perception poignant, his time metaphors often brilliant. His treatment of time also illustrated some important trends in Russian society. To be sure, his nihilist futurism of the prerevolutionary period, his cosmic-revolutionary futurism of the revolutionary period, and his utopian visions of the late 1920s were all eventually rejected by Russian society, but they remain vivid expressions of the spirit of those days.

Most of Mayakovsky's time images may be reduced to a common pattern: Mayakovsky saw Time the Preserver as enemy rather than friend. His life and his poetry were a struggle against Time's inertia, against Time the obstacle to man's ambitions. Hence Time the Destroyer became, if not exactly his friend, then certainly a welcome ally. Mayakovsky could never have exclaimed, as did his contemporary Osip Mandelshtam: "Oh, how I love the customary tread of spinning: / the shuttle scurries, and the spindle hums. . . ."[5] *Byt,* the eternal routine of everyday living, was hateful to Mayakovsky. He hated holidays, seeing them as *byt* in concentrated form: "Grab them by the gills, / and together with unsavory, dirty *byt,* // Sweep out / these holidays too" ("Summing-Up," 1929 [10:13]). Linked to this is Mayakovsky's dislike for children: the child recalls man's subjection to time, it is a hindrance to an idealized future, it means more *byt.*[6]

Mayakovsky loathed the *today.* Ideally, there existed for him only a vanquished *yesterday* and an onrushing *tomorrow.* Even Mayakovsky's positive attitude toward the future bears the mark of his negativism: he regards time not so much as the bringer of the future as that which delays it: "In savage destruction, // we shall sweep away the old, // announcing, in a thunderous voice, // a new myth to the world. // We shall kick to pieces // the fence of time" (*150,000,000* [2:125]).

Mayakovsky had no desire to meet the past on its own terms, and made no effort to understand it historically. Intentional anachronism is typical of his style, as is his pointed and provocative habit of treating Jesus Christ, Greek gods and heroes, Dante and Petrarch, Faust, Napoleon, or King Albert of Belgium—in short, every conceivable literary or historical personage—quite indiscriminately as so much material for his own puns and paradoxes. In effect, Mayakovsky does exactly what he himself satirizes in his lampoons of capitalist commercialism:

> A three digit number of years
> > has passed.
> Heroics
> > are no longer in vogue.
> Montezuma
> > has become a beer brand,
> a beer brand—Cuauhtemoc.
>
> ("Mexico," 1926 [7:45])

The point is that Mayakovsky broke with the continuity of Western civilization quite consciously. He could distinguish historical epochs, forms, and styles very well, but decided to act as though he could not and as though this were a virtue. Mayakovsky lived in an age in which nothing was stable, safe, or sacred, and he helped make it that way. His futurism, sincere in all its stages, largely coincided with the secular chiliasm of the Russian revolutionaries. They all dreamed of escaping from history, from the travail of human existence as we know it, and living in a mechanized world of things which can be manipulated with no exertion of the soul or the intellect. As Lawrence Stahlberger has pointed out, Mayakovsky chose the third of the three alternatives to the human paradox: his ideal was neither God, nor animal, but the superbly efficient machine.[7] Mayakovsky loved technological progress, the machine, and especially the flying machine. His poetry stands for everything that even today, half a century later, is considered "modern."

S. L. Frank's definition of the revolutionary faith as *"nihilist rationalism,* a combination of atheism and rejection of all objective principles by which human self-will had been checked, with a faith in human initiative which, guided by an innate striving for happiness and well-being, will easily achieve the latter solely by technological-rational organization of human activity," fits Mayakovsky's philosophy only too well.[8] Needless to say, such faith must abhor the concept of ethical or aesthetic absolutes.

In this connection, Mayakovsky's so-called "cosmism," which he shared with many of his revolutionary contemporaries, is of some interest. To be sure, Mayakovsky eventually satiricized Vadim Bayan, the self-anointed leader of "cosmism," but his own poetry remained, down to the very end, full of cosmic imagery and pregnant with the notion that, somehow, the Revolution was a cosmic phenomenon which transcended the limits of human history, the terrestrial globe, and time as we know it. How does this square with Mayakovsky's "nihilist rationalism"? Apparently, Mayakovsky and the other "cosmists" literally flee into an abstract and fantastic "cosmos" in order to escape real life, real history, and real time, all of which refute "nihilist rationalism."

To Mayakovsky the nihilist, Time the Destroyer is an ally. Much as death is welcome if it rids one of suffering, so Time the Destroyer is welcome to those who find nothing of value in the old order and ardently anticipate its destruction. Mayakovsky likes the river of time best when it flows rapidly, gathering momentum until it finally turns into a roaring deluge. Mayakovsky greets the cosmic flood of the Revolution, which would sweep away the old and clear the Earth for the new, with sincere exultation: *Mystery-Bouffe* is one of his most cheerful works.

Time the Thief is a friend and ally when it steals the capitalists' few remaining years. Time the Grave-Digger is an auspicious sight when the grave it digs is that of the bourgeoisie. In an endless chain of images, some conventional and some ingeniously original, Mayakovsky gloats at the thought of Time sweeping away, running over, and wiping out "the old." Mayakovsky's famous "March of Time" (in *The Bathhouse*) is essentially negative too:

> Forward, my country,
> > > move on faster!
> Get on with it,
> > > sweep away
> > > > old junk!
> Stronger, my commune,
> > > strike at the enemy,
> Make it die out,
> > > that monster, *byt.*
> > > (11:338)

Once again, *byt,* the business of daily living, is the devil to be exorcised. But when it comes to formulating the positive goals of the future, Mayakovsky either stops short or limits himself to such pallid generalities as that the world of the future will be free of "heartrending trivia," that health standards will be excellent, and that "life will be wholly mechanized" ("Report of the Trade Unions," 1927).

And so Mayakovsky urges Time to fly faster toward a vaguely outlined future. From here it is only a short step to the Promethean

conceit of man—Soviet man, of course—as master of Time, the
*hubris* of a man who fancies that he can seize Time by the throat
and thrust it forcibly forward. This conceit appears in some of
Mayakovsky's most daring images:

```
Enough
        of your crawling,
                        Time-the-snake,
    enough
        of your digging,
                    Time-the-mole,
    thrust of workers'
                    shock brigades,
    fling
        Time
            forward.
                    ("The Shock Workers," 1929 [10:87])
```

To be sure, this conceit was by no means specifically Mayakovskian: it was one of the most common clichés of the first full decade
of Soviet power. The slogan "The Five-Year Plan in Four Years!"
(often echoed by Mayakovsky), a kind of "realized metaphor," asserted that in the Soviet Union the impossible could and would be
accomplished. The whole phraseology of that period bore strong
overtones of man's—Soviet man's—omnipotence, his faith that he
could overcome nature, the elements, and even Time.

The notion that a rebellion against Time was a rebellion against
the laws of nature is much in evidence in Mayakovsky: the revolutionary who rejected the laws of man would not recognize the
laws of nature either. This, of course, fits in with the doctrine of
dialectical and historical materialism in its popular Soviet version,
which holds that "qualitative change" (so-called "dialectic leaps")
is inherent in all existence.

Mayakovsky was very much in step with his age, perhaps even
half a step ahead of it. While refusing to listen to the voices of
earlier ages, he had a wonderfully delicate ear for the sounds and
rhythms of his own time. Soviet scholars have sought to prove—
successfully I believe—that this quality of Mayakovsky's art was
attributable less to an intuitive empathy than to a conscious re-
sponsiveness to current events, opinions, and trends. Mayakovsky's

passionate involvement in a future-directed life, the consistency with which he pointed things, people, and ideas toward the future, the plasticity and poignancy which this theoretical future acquired in his poetry, all this made Mayakovsky the greatest, and perhaps the only, Soviet poet of his age. Others were great poets, but they were not "Soviet." Many were "Soviet," but they were no poets. Mayakovsky's desperate escapes into an ever-receding future are very deeply "Soviet," indeed.

When Mayakovsky does not look into the future, he is not at his best. In fact, it is a little embarrassing to see the great event of his lifetime, the Revolution, become a stationary beacon of inspiration, like so many historical events before it: "The October Revolution / continues, / and expands. // We live / under orders / of October's will. // Our eyes / are fixed // on the fire / of the cruiser *Aurora*" ("The Enthusiasm of Perekop," 1929 [10:8]). Mayakovsky does not seem to realize the extent to which he performs a *reductio ad absurdum* of his own Time philosophy, when he predicts that in the future, and beginning even now, old hearts will feel young again on the anniversary of the October Revolution. This presages the ghostly idea found in a Stalinist novel of later years, Vsevolod Kochetov's *Sekretar' obkoma* [The Party Secretary, 1961], that sagging party morale could be boosted by giving septuagenarian veterans of the October Revolution a greater voice in public affairs. Finally, there are moments, even for Mayakovsky, when it is not exhilarating to contemplate the action of Time the Destroyer:

> With the years, you wear out
> > the machine
> > > of your soul.
> They say:
> > It's about time
> > > to file him away,
> > > > he has written himself out!
> There's less and less love,
> > and less and less daring in me,
> and Time
> > hits me head-on,
> > > hard, on the run.
> ("Conversation with a Tax Collector about Poetry" [7:124])

### Mayakovsky the Craftsman

Mayakovsky as artist sought to keep his creative practice aligned with his theoretical pronouncements, and vice versa. More than with other major poets, his oeuvre was determined by extrinsic factors of utilitarian exigency and ideology. The futurist program shaped the early Mayakovsky's poetic practice, and later of course the program of the Russian Communist party.

Mayakovsky never renounced his allegiance to left art, and remained a spirited defender of avant-garde principles. He fought what he considered a reactionary tendency in Soviet art and literature toward reversion to nineteenth-century realist and romantic-realist forms. In a poem of 1927, "The Venus of Milo and Vyacheslav Polonsky" (in the original, a pun—something like "Venus Milosky and Vyacheslav Polonsky"), Mayakovsky puts his opponent away with the "old stuff" in the Louvre and declares his enthusiasm for Parisian Rolls-Royces and a new six-storied glass garage. As far as he is concerned, passéism is simply lazy and thoughtless hack work: "Making / *My Life for the Czar* // into *My Life for / Comrade Rykov*" ("The Hack Writer," 1928 [9:276]—Aleksey Rykov was a party functionary of some consequence). Mayakovsky's rejection of "old stuff" covered a good deal of literature that was welcomed by communist critics, including works such as Fedor Gladkov's *Tsement* [Cement] and Aleksandr Fadeev's *Razgrom* [The rout] which went on to become Soviet classics. In a satirical poem entitled "In Support of the Peoples Commissar of Public Education, Head of the Arts in the Cube, on a Burning Question, the Question about the Club" (1928), Mayakovsky announced that he would not set foot in the new writers club so long as it was a haven for "classics of literature," "red bards," and "homegrown minstrels." He also mentioned the names of writers and critics whose speeches and recitals he would rather miss. Among them were Leopold Averbakh and Sergey Rodov, leading ideologues of RAPP, and Aleksey Tolstoy and Vsevolod Ivanov, major Soviet "classics" in the realist tradition.

Mayakovsky's utilitarianism was accompanied by a pointedly modern, constructivist understanding of the creative process. "I study every word and the effect on the reader which I want to produce by it, exactly the way the people who write your advertisements do," he explained to an American journalist. In an explicit declaration of his utilitarian aesthetics, "Homeward Bound" (1925), Mayakovsky eventually dropped this powerful quatrain:

> I want to be understood by my country,
> but if I'm not, so what?
> I'll pass by to the side, on my way through my own country,
> as a slanting rain passes.
>
> (7:429)

The image here is drawn from a formulaic expression denoting the passing of a rain cloud to the side. Mayakovsky called this quatrain a "bird of paradise tail feather" which he plucked out on account of its "romancy sentimentality" (7:489). This means he would sacrifice even a magnificent passage to maintain his image as a dedicated but wholly unsentimental craftsman.

Mayakovsky was, however, quite sensitive to any challenge to his craftsmanship. During the last years of his life he responded often and vigorously to charges that his poetry was "coarse," "superficial," "unintelligible to the masses," and so on. Mayakovsky boasted that his verses were "palpable, coarse, visible" ("At the Top of My Voice"), and indeed concreteness was a significant trait of his work from the beginning. He always liked to talk about real places, real events, and real people, whom he called by their real names: Lilya and Osya Brik, "Roma" Jakobson, Esenin, Comrade Nette, and innumerable others. And, of course, Vladimir Mayakovsky. David Burlyuk remarked quite correctly that everything in Mayakovsky's poetry was autobiographical. Mayakovsky was fully aware of this tendency: "But today, / pieces of literature / are made / thus: // The writer / takes a fact, // living / and vibrant. // Not so he might recognize himself / in some anonymous character. // He writes, / bandying his heroes about. // If he's a hero— / let's have his name! / / If he's scum— / put down his address!" ("We are Writers," 1928 [9:111]).

Mayakovsky's striving for concreteness has many facets. His refusal to use conventional poetic language is one of them. His effort to keep his rhythms close to those of ordinary speech is another. Yet another is his consistent use of highly distinctive imagery. His personal view of things fits this pattern: more often than not Vladimir Mayakovsky is Mayakovsky's poetic persona. Mayakovsky's acceptance of the "factography" principle fits this pattern: "I won't consider / the best pieces of poetic fame // the equal of // a simple / newspaper fact" ("The Best Verse," 1927 [8:60]).

We have, then, a deep contradiction which permeates Mayakovsky's aesthetics as well as his poetics. There is, on the one hand, a pointed striving for concreteness, one by no means limited to Mayakovsky's Soviet period, much less to his propaganda verse. But on the other hand, there is his equally pointed dislike of psychological motivation or psychological analysis, his simplistic treatment of social and political phenomena, and his cavalier attitude toward the very facts to which he attributed so much importance. The resolution of this contradiction is identical for Mayakovsky's pre- and postrevolutionary verse, as well as for his civic and personal verse. What is highly concrete—"realistic," if you wish—is his form, the details of his language and imagery. The content—emotional, social, or political—is pointedly subjective in the prerevolutionary and personal poetry, and pointedly slanted in the postrevolutionary "civic" poetry.

In some ways Mayakovsky's poetics contradicts the traditions and conventions of lyric poetry. It eschews poetic language, formulaic diction, and conventional imagery. While lyric poetry traditionally tends toward the vague and even the obscure, Mayakovsky's poetry is pointed, concrete, and palpable. While lyric poetry conventionally gravitates toward symbols and tends toward ambiguity, Mayakovsky's images are usually allegoric, while his similes and metaphors are pure conceits, without a symbolic connotation. In these areas Mayakovsky's poetics follow the pattern of classicism, instead of the essentially romantic poetics of most of his Russian contemporaries.

## The Ethics of a Revolutionary Aesthetic

Mayakovsky's ethics differ as much from those of any major poet of his age as his aesthetics. Here too there is a certain continuity between Mayakovsky the futurist and Mayakovsky the Soviet poet. The Nietzschean amoralism of his prerevolutionary work is channeled into the ruthlessness of the political agitator. The values of the futurist are entirely subjective, that is, ethically neutral. Mayakovsky the futurist is an ethical nihilist. Religious and other values are for him no more than artistic raw material. Mayakovsky as political agitator converts his ethical nihilism into a communist virtue. Pasternak's description in *Doctor Zhivago* of the Russian intellectual who abrogates his right to independent thought because he thinks it morally purer to work for the cause uncritically surely applies to Mayakovsky. It is inconceivable that a man of Mayakovsky's intelligence could have been blind to the blatant failings of the regime he wholeheartedly supported. Everything we know about him indicates that he was an honest man and no coward. Hence he must have felt that the regime deserved his unconditional loyalty despite its lies, its injustices, and its cruelties. Anyway, Mayakovsky could exhibit a veritable pogrom mentality when he denounced the regime's enemies, internal and external. When he visited Sverdlovsk (formerly Ekaterinburg) in January 1928, he wrote poems hailing the success of the industrialization program in the Urals, but also found time to write a poem entitled "The Emperor" mocking the memory of the czar and his family who had been murdered there. And in general Mayakovsky's political poetry reflects the meanness in the treatment of a defeated enemy that is so characteristic of the Soviet regime, as witness his treatment of the routed and persecuted socialist revolutionaries in "This Tale about the Peregrinations of an S. R. around the World" (1924), or aging émigrés in Paris ("At 12 O'Clock P.M.," 1929).

Even worse are poems one cannot help calling rhymed denunciations. A poem of 1927 attacking Professor Georgy Shengeli, with whom Mayakovsky carried on a running battle for several years, "My Speech at the Public Trial Occasioned by a Possible Scandal at a Lecture of Professor Shengeli," includes these lines: "I can see through this whole thing, // I know whose copy these people are. // In their songs / the ritual of the church is alive, // they are / rhymed opium" (8:29). The point of the poem is that Professor Shengeli encourages poetry that is as good as prayer and promotes the transformation of Young Communists into deacons. Though these are, of course, metaphors, and Mayakovsky wants to say that the poet is not a "seer," "prophet," or "visionary," but a craftsman, he still must have known that his denunciation might have dire consequences for his opponent. A poem of 1928, "Each His Own Central Executive Committee," denounces the local party organization in Tambov for having reduced a counterrevolutionary's ten-year sentence to two-and-a-half years. Mayakovsky's antireligious propaganda is always vicious, particularly considering that it is directed against a prostrate and cruelly persecuted foe. Two out of many examples are "The Priest" (1928), a particularly unpleasant mockery of a helpless opponent, and "On How Certain Sectarians Invite Workers to Dances" (1928), in which Russian Baptists are presented as a front for American dollar imperialism.

It is characteristic of Mayakovsky that he should have used the occasion of the 100th anniversary of Tolstoy's birth to denounce those who follow Tolstoy's teaching of nonviolence—except "if it happens not here, but abroad" ("Vegetarians," 1928 [9:309]). Quite consistently with this, Mayakovsky eulogizes Feliks Dzerzhinsky, infamous head of the Cheka (secret police) and later of the GPU ("Letter of the Writer Vladimir Vladimirovich Mayakovsky to the Writer Aleksey Maksimovich Gorky," 1926). In a word, Mayakovsky embraced the new morality based on absolute loyalty to the Soviet state and the Communist party and callous disregard of traditional values. The following lines from *Vladimir Ilich Lenin* exemplify this: "I want to let shine anew // that majestic word, 'the party.' // The individual. / Who needs him?! // The voice of the individual / is thinner than a squeal. // Who will ever hear it?— / His wife, maybe. // And that, / only if it isn't at the market, / but nearby" (6:265). And Mayakovsky continues to mock the individual's powerlessness and isolation.

Mayakovsky's allegiance to Soviet morality was uncompromising and consistent. He was ruthless in his attacks on those whom the regime defined as its enemies, and on some of his own as well. Such ruthlessness was then considered a virtue, and Mayakovsky's enemies, especially the critics of RAPP, were, if anything, even more ruthless than he. A Western reader must recall that what to him seems insidious slander based on patent falsehoods, was the official party line of the 1920s. The question of whether Mayakovsky believed in these falsehoods is irrelevant, for it seems clear that he was honest in his allegiance to the Soviet regime. Mayakovsky subordinated any "subjective" truth to the higher, "objective" truth of the party line.

In speaking of Mayakovsky's last public appearances, which were marred by heckling and stupid questions, Edward J. Brown comments: "the record of this incident in Moscow contains in little the full tragedy of a poet misunderstood and rejected during his own lifetime both by those he wanted to reject him and by those he wanted to accept him."[9] Besides this sympathetic assessment, one should mention also the reaction of those who were unwilling to accept Mayakovsky. Vladislav Khodasevich (1886–1939), a major émigré poet and critic, said in an essay written a week after Mayakovsky's suicide that Mayakovsky had merely gotten his just deserts. He had, said Khodasevich, given the street mob what it wanted: "The riches accumulated by human thought, he dragged out into the marketplace, trivializing the refined, oversimplifying the complex, coarsening the subtle, making the profound shallow, and belittling and vilifying the sublime."[10] Khodasevich conceded that Mayakovsky had displayed extraordinary talent in so doing, but a talent at producing nonpoetry skillfully masquerading as poetry. Mayakovsky, said Khodasevich, was richly rewarded for his efforts by party bosses masquerading as revolutionaries, who "proclaimed him a poet of the Revolution and even pretended to believe in the revolutionary biography which he had invented for himself." All of this, Khodasevich concluded, was bound to catch up with Mayakovsky, as he "exhausted the modest arsenal of his possibilities" and was left with nothing new to offer even to the young generation of Soviet poets.

Khodasevich's harsh words were also just: Mayakovsky had been no kinder to the memory of Aleksandr Blok. Khodasevich's judgment derives from two assumptions, neither of which can be verified. The first is that "crudity and baseness may be the subject of poetry, but not its inner motor, nor its true content." Mayakovsky was the author of many skillfully composed verses whose thrust was unequivocally that of a pogrom. If moral criteria should be applied to poetry, these verses were indeed nonpoetry, as Khodasevich claimed. The second is that there was no excuse for Mayakovsky's vicious attacks on defenseless enemies and his obsequious service to a cruel regime. The defense against this is, of course, that Mayakovsky may not have seen things that way.

## Posterity's Assessment

An assessment of Mayakovsky the poet cannot be based on a separation between his "genuine poetry" and his "propaganda poetry." Like most artists, Mayakovsky matured and became more skillful at his craft as he grew older. A good deal of his "Soviet" poetry is technically superior to the best of his prerevolutionary verse. It makes even less sense to glean from Mayakovsky's oeuvre those lines which can be readily accepted as "poetry" according to nineteenth-century norms, for these are not always his best lines. "Past One O'Clock" is a case in point: though certainly "poetry" by nineteenth-century standards, it is rather mediocre. Nor is it true that Mayakovsky's "personal" poetry is always better than his "propaganda" poetry. "A Letter to Comrade Kostrov from Paris, on the Nature of Love" is by no means superior to, say, "Verses on My Soviet Passport." We must accept or reject Mayakovsky as a whole, though our evaluation is made difficult by several factors. It is not easy to dismiss from one's mind Mayakovsky's flamboyant and generally attractive personality, his "poetic life," as Pasternak put it. Nor can Mayakovsky's histrionic talents, his brilliant delivery of his poetry, and his spirited defense of his own work be dismissed as irrelevant to the question of his poetic worth: these things certainly contributed to his great stature among his contemporaries. Furthermore, Mayakovsky was the acknowledged leader of a school. He did not invent any of the truly innovative tenets of Russian futurism, but since Khlebnikov, Kruchonykh, and Kamensky, bolder innovators than Mayakovsky, never acquired anything approaching his fame, he received most of the credit for the achievements of that school.

Soviet critics and scholars have suggested that Mayakovsky created a new aesthetic by transferring the viewpoint of lyric poetry from a personal to a social stance, by "poeticizing man the creator of his social existence,"[11] or by creating a "new poetic 'I' where the 'I' is grandiose, but not with a romantic grandioseness, by which an exalted 'I' is juxtaposed to a lowly world of reality, but a different grandioseness which encompasses the whole world and feels responsible for it."[12] But surely in this respect Mayakovsky is anything but unique. His stance—whether one calls it "social," "collective," "civic," or something else—often recalls, *mutatis mutandis,* that of the poets of classicism as well as of Nekrasov and other civic poets of the nineteenth century. Osip Mandelshtam, a keen judge of talent, recognized the basically didactic quality of Mayakovsky's poetry:

Mayakovsky's merit lies in his using the powerful resources of visual education to educate the masses. Like a schoolteacher, Mayakovsky carries a globe representing the Earth, and other emblems of the visual method, with him at all times. He has replaced the repulsive newspaper of recent times, where nobody could understand a thing, with simple, healthy school work. A great reformer of the newspaper, he has left a deep mark on poetic language, having greatly simplified syntax and assigned to the noun a place of honor and primacy in the sentence.[13]

Mandelshtam is thinking of *Mystery-Bouffe* here, but the context suggests that he speaks of Mayakovsky in general.

To be sure, Mayakovsky's message was modern. Pasternak recalled that Mayakovsky once said to him: "Well, sure enough. You and I are different, indeed. You like lightning in the sky, and I like it in an electric iron."[14] While didactic poetry was nothing new, didactic poetry dealing with the construction of hydroelectric power plants was.

Perhaps the most innovative aspect of Mayakovsky's poetry was that a poet of his remarkable talent could devote almost all his energies to the production of utilitarian pieces, many of them utterly banal. Mayakovsky did not see in this any "death of poetry," but rather a recapturing of its proper social role. In this regard, the position of Mayakovsky the Soviet poet was diametrically opposed to that of Mayakovsky the futurist, who had advocated a poetry of pure form.

Mayakovsky has influenced more Soviet poets, Russian and non-Russian, than any other twentieth-century poet, partly because Soviet youth has been exposed to his poetry vastly more than to the work of his contemporaries Pasternak, Mandelshtam, Akhmatova, Tsvetaeva, and Zabolotsky, all of whom may have been greater poets than he. Furthermore, like Pushkin, Mayakovsky had a "galaxy" of sorts. Nikolay Aseev (1889–1963), a faithful friend and collaborator, not only continued writing poetry very much in Mayakovsky's manner (only a bit tamer and neater) for thirty years after his friend's death, but also produced a lengthy verse epic, *Incipit Mayakovsky* (1937–50), devoted to his life and works. Aseev's *poema* not only quotes Mayakovsky often, directly and indirectly, but also echoes his rhythms and duplicates his mannerisms. Semyon Kirsanov (1906–72)—a talented disciple of Mayakovsky's and a poet of some originality of thought if not of form—wrote sharply pointed topical poetry in the Mayakovskian vein for several decades, and toward the end of his life devoted a good many poems to cosmic themes, which was reminiscent of Mayakovsky. There were lesser poetic disciples, and also several *littérateurs* who devoted their lives to the propagation of the memory and works of the master: Vasily Kamensky, who celebrated the memory of his friend in verse and in prose, Osip Brik, Viktor Pertsov, and V. A. Katanyan.

When Soviet literature emerged from the doldrums of Stalin's last years, the generation of young poets who restored some life to it quite naturally wrote in the style of Mayakovsky, a style that was accessible, relatively easy, and well suited for public recitals, which once again became popular in the late 1950s. The poetic style of Evgeny Evtushenko, Boris Slutsky, Robert Rozhdestvensky, Leonid Martynov, and Yury Kuznetsov, to mention but a few, was certainly modeled on Mayakovsky's.

Mayakovsky has held a strong attraction for poets of the leftist avant-garde everywhere. Bertolt Brecht and Johannes R. Becher in Germany, Paul Eluard and Louis Aragon in France, Wladysław Broniewski and Witold Wandurski in Poland, S. K. Neumann in Czechoslovakia, Pablo Neruda among several Latin American poets, and many others have expressed their appreciation of Mayakovsky's art and acknowledged his influence on their own work.

While Mayakovsky's style has stood up well under the wear and tear of time, and while his utilitarian aesthetic is very much alive, his poetry has been "dated" for a long time. While the verses of Pasternak or Mandelshtam are as fresh and fascinating today as they were sixty years ago, one reads Mayakovsky's for their historical and technical interest rather than for aesthetic enjoyment. Mayakovsky's prediction that his verses would reach the future much the way a Roman aqueduct has reached us has come true.

# Notes and References

*Chapter One*

1. Vladimir Mayakovskii, *Polnoe sobranie sochinenii,* 13 vols. (Moscow, 1955–62), 10:279; hereafter cited in the text by volume and page.
2. V. Katanyan, *Mayakovskii: Literaturnaya khronika* (Moscow: Sovetskii pisatel', 1948), pp. 34–35.
3. A concert piece by Rakhmaninov, conceivably inspired by Arnold Böcklin's painting of the same title. "The Isle of the Dead" remained for Mayakovsky a symbol of sentimental philistinism posing as art.
4. Shakhno Epstein, "Vstrechi s Vladimirom Mayakovskim" [Encounters with Vladimir Mayakovsky], *Chervonii shlyakh* [Red Road] nos. 5–6, (1930), p. 149.

*Chapter Two*

1. Yet the "decadent" Symbolist Fedor Sologub also railed against the sun as the source of an accursed earthly existence and the origin of evil, and this as early as 1907, in a volume entitled *Zmii* [Serpents]. One could go much further back and find similar motifs in romantic titanism, Shelley's, for example. The difference between *décadence* and futurism is one of emphasis.
2. "The Relation of Today's Theatre and Cinema to Art" (1913), a paper which shows Mayakovsky to have been well up in the art theory of the day.
3. I. Kostovskii, *Mayakovskii i mirovaya poeziya* [Mayakovsky and World Poetry] (Washington, D.C.: Victor Kamkin, 1974), pp. 82–83.
4. Viktor Shklovskii, *Zhili-byli* [Once upon a time] (Moscow, 1966), p. 296.
5. Lawrence Leo Stahlberger, *The Symbolic System of Majakovskij* (The Hague: Mouton, 1964), p. 62.

*Chapter Three*

1. Petr Nikolaevich Wrangel (1878–1928), commander of a counter-revolutionary army in southern Russia in 1920.

2. Is it coincidental that the meter of this poem coincides with that of Goethe's ballad "Die wandelnde Glocke," which features a similar theme (a church bell leaving its belltower to admonish a lazy churchgoer)?

3. F. N. Pitskel', *Mayakovskii: Khudozhestvennoe postizhenie mira* [Mayakovsky: his creative understanding of the world] (Moscow, 1979), p. 151.

*Chapter Four*

1. See Halina Stephan, *Lef and the Left Front of the Arts* (Munich, 1981), p. 53.

2. *Lef* 1, no. 5 (1925).

3. See Lars Kleberg, "Notes on the Poem *Vladimir Il'ich Lenin,*" in *Vladimir Majakovskij: Memoirs and Essays,* ed. Bengt Jangfeldt and Nils Åke Nilsson (Stockholm, 1975), pp. 167–69.

4. See Nina Tumarkin, "Religion, Bolshevism, and the Origins of the Lenin Cult," *Russian Review* 40 (1981):35–46.

5. The quotation is from Pitskel', *Mayakovskii,* p. 192.

6. Much as the hero of Dostoevsky's utopian fantasy "Dream of a Ridiculous Man" (1877).

7. A major river in Central Russia.

*Chapter Five*

1. For more on Mayakovsky's rhymes, see Edward J. Brown, *Mayakovsky: A Poet in the Revolution* (Princeton, 1973), p. 173. Of course Mayakovsky did not invent the punning rhyme. A nineteenth-century satirical poet, Dmitry Minaev (1835–89), in some ways a precursor of Mayakovsky, also produced some ingenious punning rhymes.

2. Stahlberger, *Symbolic System,* pp. 14, 61–63, 141.

3. Assya Humesky, *Majakovskij and His Neologisms* (New York, 1964).

4. *Pravda,* 14 April 1940, quoted by Pitskel', *Mayakovskii,* p. 333.

5. Osip Mandel'shtam, *Tristia,* in *Sobranie sochinenii* [Collected works] (Washington, D.C.: Inter-Language Literary Associates, 1964), 1:73.

6. This detail was first noted by Roman Jakobson. See Stahlberger, *Symbolic System,* p. 119.

7. See ibid., p. 144.

8. S. L. Frank, "Religiozno-istoricheskii smysl russkoy revolyutsii" [The religious and historical meaning of the Russian Revolution], in *Mosty: Sbornik statey k 50-letiyu russkoy revolyutsii* [Bridges: a collection of articles to mark the 50th anniversary of the Russian Revolution] (Munich, 1967), pp. 15–16.

9. Brown, *Mayakovsky,* p. 26.

10. Vladislav Khodasevich, "O Mayakovskom" [On Mayakovsky], in *Literaturnye stat'i i vospominaniya* [Literary articles and reminiscences] (New York: Chekhov Publishing House, 1954), pp. 219–32.

11. Nikolay Aseev, as quoted by Pitskel', *Mayakovskii,* p. 335.

12. Boris Eikhenbaum, as quoted in ibid., p. 353.

13. Osip Mandel'shtam, "Burya i natisk" [Storm and stress], in *Sobranie sochinenii* [Collected works] (N.p., 1966), 2:391–92.

14. Boris Pasternak, "Lyudi i polozheniya: Avtobiograficheskii ocherk" [People and situations: an autobiographical sketch], *Novyi mir* [New world], no. 1 (1967), p. 230.

# Selected Bibliography

Darring, Gerald. "Mayakovsky: A Bibliography of Criticism (1912–1930)." *Russian Literature Triquarterly*, no. 2 (1972), pp. 510–29. Darring's bibliography is extensive and lists earlier bibliographies.

Lewanski, Richard C., comp. *The Literature of the World in English Translation: A Bibliography*. Vol. 2. *The Slavic Literatures*. New York: Frederick Ungar, 1967, pp. 302–4. Bibliography of English translations.

## PRIMARY SOURCES

The Russian text referred to in this book is Vladimir Mayakovskii, *Polnoe sobranie sochinenii* [Complete Works], 13 vols. (Moscow: Goslitizdat, 1955–62). It was, at the time of the writing of this book, the authoritative edition of Mayakovsky's works. It gives textual variants and has a commentary containing historical and literary facts concerning the genesis, the background, and the text of each work. In part 1, below, I have given the source in the *Complete Works*.

1. Poetry and Other Writings

*About That* (1923)—*Pro eto*, 4:135.

"About Trash" (1920)—"O dryani," 2:73.

"Alarm" (1930)—"Trevoga," 10:165.

*America* (cycle of poems, 1925–26)—*Stikhi ob Amerike*, 7:7–92.

"Americans are Surprised" (1929)—"Amerikantsy udivlyayutsya," 10:89.

"Anniversary Poem" (1924)—"Yubileynoe," 6:47.

"Answer to Future Gossip, An" (1928)—"Otvet na budushchie spletni, 9:390.

"Appeal" (1927)—"Prizyv," 8:135.

"At the Top of My Voice" (1930)—"Vo ves' golos: Pervoe vstuplenie v poemu," 10:279.

"At 12 O'Clock P.M." (1929)—"V 12 chasov po nocham," 10:105.

"Automobile Ride, An" (1913)—"V avto," 1:58.

*Backbone Flute, The* (1915)—*Fleyta-pozvonochnik*, 1:197.

"Ballad about Emile the Valiant" (1922)—"Ballada o doblestnom Emile," 4:38.
"Ballad about the Bureaucrat" (1928)—"Ballada o byurokrate i rabkore," 9:269.
*Bathhouse, The* (play, 1930)—*Banya,* 11:277.
*Bedbug, The* (play, 1929)—*Klop,* 11:215.
"Best Verse, The" (1927)—"Luchshii stikh," 8:59.
"Black and White" (1925)—"Blek end uayt," 7:20.
"Bolt your pineapple" (1917)—"Esh' ananasy," 1:148.
"Bonebreakers and Butchers" (1928)—"Kostolomy i myasniki," 9:252.
"Broadway" (1925)—"Brodvey," 7:55.
"Brooklyn Bridge" (1925)—"Bruklinskii most," 7:83.
"But Could You?" (1913)—"A vy mogli by?" 1:40.

"Camp 'Nit Gedajge' " (1925)—"Kemp 'Nit gedajge,' " 7:88.
"Case of the Bandleader, The" (1915)—"Koe-chto po povodu dirizhora," 1:90.
"Challenge, A" (1925)—"Vyzov," 7:73.
"Children's Theatre, The" (1928)—"Detskii teatr," 9:65.
"Christopher Columbus" (1925)—"Khristofor Kolomb," 7:31.
"Cinema and Vodka" (1928)—"Kino i vino," 9:64.
"Civilian Shrapnel" (article, 1914)—"Shtatskaya shrapnel'," 1:302.
*Cloud in Trousers, A* (1915)—*Oblako v shtanakh,* 1:173.
"Comintern" (1923)—"Komintern," 5:73.
"Comrade Typist" (1927)—"Tovarishchu mashinistke," 8:92.
"Comrades, Shall We Ever See Good Housing?" (1928)—"Dozhdyomsya li my zhil'ya khoroshego? Tovarishchi, stroyte khorosho i dyoshevo!" 9:203.
"Conversation with a Tax Collector about Poetry" (1926)—"Razgovor s fininspektorom o poezii," 7:119.
"Coward, The" (1928)—"Trus," 9:209.
"Crimea, The" (1927)—"Krym," 8:144.
"Criticism of Selfcriticism" (1929)—"Kritika samokritiki," 9:130.
"Cross and Champagne, A" (1928)—"Krest i shampanskoe," 9:187.

"Darkness" (1916)—"Mrak," 1:118.
"Decent Citizen, A" (1925)—"Poryadochnyi grazhdanin," 7:70.
*Dekabryukhov and Oktyabryukhov* (film, 1928)—*Dekabryukhov i Oktyabryukhov,* 11:113.
"Don't Do Business with Lenin!" (1924)—"Ne torguyte Leninym!"
"Don't Get Carried Away" (1929)—"Ne uvlekaytes' nami," 10:155.
"Down with Whites and Greens" (1928)—"Bey belykh i zelyonykh," 9:87.

"Hypocrite, The" (1928)—"Khanzha," 9:367.

*I* (cycle of verse, 1913)—"Ya," 1:45–49.
"I and Napoleon" (1915)—"Ya i Napoleon," 1:72.
"Idyl" (1928)—"Idilliya," 9:340.
"I Love" (1922)—"Lyublyu," 4:83.
"In Search of Socks" (1928)—"Poiski noskov," 9:324.
"In Support of the Peoples Commissar of Public Education" (1928)—
    "Pomoshch' Narkomprosu, Glaviskusstvu v kube," 9:256.
"I Testify" (1926)—"Svidetel'stvuyu," 7:58.
"Ivan Ivanovich Gonorarchikov" (1927)—"Ivan Ivanovich Gonorarchi-
    kov," 8:165.

"Jaurès" (1925)—"Zhores," 6:219.

*Lady and the Hooligan, The* (film, 1918)—*Baryshnya i khuligan,* 11:482.
"La Parisienne" (1929)—"Parizhanka," 10:63.
"Left March" (1918)—"Levyi marsh," 2:23.
"Leninists, The" (1930)—"Lenintsy," 10:171.
"Let's Have a Material Base" (1929)—"Dayosh' material'nuyu bazu!"
    10:147.
"Let's Have Automobiles!" (1928)—"Dayosh' avtomobil'," 9:315.
"Let's Have Some Rotten Eggs!" (1928)—"Dayosh' tukhlye yaytsa!" 9:56.
"Let's Take Our New Rifles" (1925)—"Voz'myom vintovki novye," 10:264.
"Let's Vote 'Uninterrupted'!" (1929)—"Golosuem za nepreryvku," 10:77.
"Letter from the Writer Vladimir Vladimirovich Mayakovsky to the Writer
    Aleksey Maksimovich Gorky" (1927)—"Pis'mo pisatelya Vladimira
    Vladimirovicha Mayakovskogo pisatelyu Alekseyu Maksimovichu
    Gor'komu," 7:206.
"Letter to Comrade Kostrov from Paris, On the Nature of Love" (1928)—
    "Pis'mo tovarishchu Kostrovu iz Parizha o sushchnosti lyubvi," 9:381.
"Letter to Tatyana Yakovleva" (1928)—"Pis'mo Tat'yane Yakovlevoy,"
    9:386.
"Lickspittle, The" (1928)—"Podliza," 9:359.
"Listen, If They Light Stars" (1913)—"Poslushayte!" 1:60.

*Man* (1916–17)—*Chelovek,* 1:243.
"March of Shock Brigades" (1930)—"Marsh udarnykh brigad," 10:162.
"March of the Twenty-Five Thousand" (1930)—"Marsh dvadtsati pyati
    tysyach," 10:176.
"Marusya Poisoned Herself" (1927)—"Marusya otravilas'," 8:188.
"Marxism is a Weapon" (1928)—"Marksizm—oruzhie," 7:106.
"Mexico" (1926)—"Meksika," 7:41 (poem), 7:347 (travel sketch).

"Miss and Woolworth's, The" (1925)—"Baryshnya i Vul'vort," 7:62.
"Monte Carlo" (1929)—"Monte-Karlo," 10:47.
"Moscow on Fire (1905)" (play, 1930)—"Moskva gorit," 11:355, 383.
"Most Important Bit of Advice to a Housewife, A" (1928)—"Vazhneyshii sovet domashney khozyayke," 9:259.
*My Discovery of America* (travelogue, 1925–26)—*Moyo otkrytie Ameriki,* 7:265.
"My Speech at a Public Trial occasioned by a Possible Scandal at a Lecture by Professor Shengeli" (1927)—"Moya rech' na pokazatel'nom protsesse po sluchayu vozmozhnogo skandala s lektsiyami professora Shengeli," 8:27.
"My Speech at the Genoa Conference" (1922)—"Moya rech' na genuezskoy konferentsii," 4:27.
*Mystery-Bouffe* (play, 1918)—*Misteriya-buff,* 2:167, 243.

"Note to China, A" (1929)—"Nota Kitayu," 10:72.
*Not for Money Born* (film, 1918)—*Ne dlya deneg rodivshiisya,* 11:481.
"Notre Dame" (1925)—"Notre-Dame," 6:211.

*150,000,000* (1920–21)—*150,000,000,* 2:113.
"On How Certain Sectarians Invite Workers to Dances" (1928)—"O tom, kak nekie sektanttsy zovut rabochego na tantsy," 9:193.
"On Pedestrians and Jaywalkers" (1928)—"Pro peshekhodov i razin'," 9:206.
"Open Letter to the Workers" (manifesto, 1918)—"Otkrytoe pis'mo rabochim," 12:8.
"Order No. 2 to the Army of the Arts" (1921)—"Prikaz No. 2 armii iskusstv," 2:86.
"Order to the Army of the Arts" (1918)—"Prikaz po armii iskusstva," 2:14.
"Our March" (1918)—"Nash marsh," 2:7.

"Painting of Today, The" (article, 1914)—"Zhivopis' segodnyashnego dnya," 1:286.
"Paris" (1923)—"Parizh," 4:205.
*Paris* (cycle of poems, 1925)—*Parizh,* 6:195–227.
"Party Candidates" (1929)—"Kandidat iz partii," 10:45.
"Peasant Affairs" (1924)—"Krest'yanskoe," 6:164.
"Pillar of Society, The" (1928)—"Stolp," 9:343.
"Poem on Clothes and Youth, A" (1930)—"Stikhotvorenie odezhno-molodyozhnoe," 10:160.
"Poet-Worker, The" (1918)—"Poet rabochii," 2:18.
"Priest, The" (1928)—"Pop," 9:357.

"Propaganda and Advertising" (article, 1923)—"Agitatsiya i reklama," 12:57.

"Quick Glance at the Vernissages, A" (article, 1914)—"Begom cherez vernisazhi," 1:340.

"Red Arabs" (1928)—"Krasnye arapy," 9:100.

"Relation of Today's Theater and Cinema to Art, The" (1913)—"Otnoshenie segodnyashnego teatra i kinematografa k iskusstvu," 1:281.

"Report of the Trade Unions" (1927)—"Raport profsoyuzov," 8:203.

"Revolution: A Poetic Chronicle" (1917)—"Revolyutsiya—Poetokhronika," 1:134.

"Rime about Trash and Petty Trash" (1928)—"Stikh ne pro dryan', a pro dryantso," 9:219.

*ROSTA Windows* (1919–21)—*Okna satiry ROSTA*, 3:7–434.

"Rural Correspondent, The" (1924)—"Sel'kor," 6:92.

"Seaport, A" (1912)—"Port," 1:36.

"Separate Opinion, A" (1929)—"Osoboe mnenie," 10:138.

"Shkafolyubov's Love" (film, 1928)—"Lyubov' Shkafolyubova," 11:91.

"Shockworkers, The" (1929)—"Zastrel'shchiki," 10:87.

"Six Nuns" (1925)—"6 monakhin'," 7:9.

"Sky-Scraper, The: A Cross Section" (1925)—"Neboskryob v razreze," 7:66.

"Soviet Alphabet" (1919)—"Sovetskaya azbuka," 2:92.

"Strange . . . but True" (1928)—"Stranno . . . no verno," 9:191.

"Summing-Up" (1929)—"Itogi," 10:12.

"Swine!" (1922)—"Svolochi," 4:14.

"Syphilis" (1925)—"Sifilis," 7:24.

"Tale about Petya, a Fat Child, and Sima, a Thin One" (1925)—"Skazka o Pete, tolstom rebyonke, i o Sime, kotoryi tonkii," 10:217.

"Tale about the Peregrinations of an S. R. around the World" (1924)— "Povestvovanie eto o stranstvii esera vokrug sveta," 6:173.

"Tale of the Deserter, Who Set Himself Up Pretty Good" (1920)—"Skazka o dezertire, ustroivshemsya nedurnen'ko," 2:49.

"There!" (1914)—"Nate!" 1:56.

"Third Internationale, The" (1920)—"III Internatsional," 2:43.

"To All" (1916)—"Ko vsemu," 1:103.

"To Avoid Intellectual Controversy" (1928)—"Vo izbezhanie umstvennykh brozhenii," 9:346.

"To Comrade Nette" (1926)—"Tovarishchu Nette," 7:162.

"To Himself, Beloved" (1916)—"Sebe lyubimomu," 1:126.

"Without White Flags" (essay, 1914)—"Bez belykh flagov," 1:321.
"Wrecker, The" (1928)—"Vreditel'," 9:157.

"Yid" (1928)—"Zhid," 9:116.
"Young Communist, The" (1924)—"Komsomol'skaya," 6:34.

2. English Translations

*The Bedbug and Selected Poetry.* Edited by Patricia Blake, translated by Max Hayward and George Reavey. Cleveland: World Publishing Co., 1960.

*The Complete Plays.* Translated by Guy Daniels, introduction by Robert Payne. New York: Washington Square Press, 1968.

*Electric Iron.* Translated by Jack Hirshman and Victor Erlich. Berkeley: Maya, 1971.

*How Are Verses Made?* Translated by G. M. Hyde. London: J. Cape, 1970.

*Mayakovsky and his Poetry.* Compiled and translated by Herbert Marshall. 3d ed. Bombay: Current Book House, 1955.

*Mayakovsky.* Translated and edited by Herbert Marshall. New York: Hill and Wang, 1965.

*Selected Poetry.* Translated by Dorian Rottenberg. Moscow: Progress Publishers, 1972.

"Two Mayakovsky Scenarios." Introduction by Peter Wollen. *Screen* 12, no. 4 (Winter 1971–72):122–49.

*Vladimir Ilyich Lenin.* Translated by Dorian Rottenberg. Moscow: Progress Publishers, 1976.

3. Books with Reproductions of Mayakovsky's Art Work

Antelme, Marie Laure, ed. *Maïakovski: 20 ans de travail* [Mayakovsky: 20 years of work]. Paris, 1975. Exhibition catalog. Exhibition at the Centre national d'art contemporain in Paris, 18 November 1975– 5 January 1976.

Majakovskij, Vladimir. *Vers und Hammer: Schriften, Gedichte, Zeichnungen, Photos, Dokumente* [Verse and hammer: writings, poems, drawings, photos, documents]. Zürich: Die Arche, 1959.

*Majakovskij: 20 Jahre Arbeit* [Mayakovsky: 20 years of work]. Edited by Eckhart Gillen. 2d ed. Berlin: NGBK, 1978. Catalog of exhibition held in 1978.

SECONDARY SOURCES

Barooshian, Vahan D. *Brik and Mayakovsky.* The Hague: Mouton, 1978. An account of their personal and literary relationships.

————. *Russian Cubo-Futurism 1910–1930: A Study in Avant-Gardism*. The Hague: Mouton, 1974. A survey of the history and aesthetics of Russian futurism.

Bowlt, John E. *Russian Art of the Avant-Garde: Theory and Criticism 1902–1934*. New York: Viking, 1976. Relevant for the connection of futurism with the visual arts.

Brown, Edward J. *Mayakovsky: A Poet in the Revolution*. Princeton: Princeton University Press, 1973. By far the best "life and works" type book on Mayakovsky in any language.

Charters, Anna, and Charters, Samuel. *I love: The Story of Vladimir Mayakovsky and Lili Brik*. New York: Farrar, Straus & Giroux, 1979. Relevant to one aspect of Mayakovsky's biography.

Eventov, Isaak. *Mayakovskii-plakatist: Kriticheskii ocherk* [Mayakovsky's posters: a critical essay]. Leningrad: Iskusstvo, 1940. A monograph on Mayakovsky the cartoonist and graphic artist.

Fleyshman, Lazar'. *Boris Pasternak v dvadtsatye gody* [Boris Pasternak in the 1920s]. Munich: Wilhelm Fink, n.d. [1980?]. Highly relevant for Mayakovsky's literary struggles and alliances in the 1920s.

Gasparov, Mikhail. *Sovremennyi russkii stikh: Metrika i ritmika* [Contemporary Russian verse: metrics and rhythmics]. Moscow: Nauka, 1974. Much of this book is devoted to Mayakovsky's versification.

Humesky, Assya. *Majakovskij and His Neologisms*. New York: Rausen, 1964. An exhaustive treatment of Mayakovsky's neologisms.

Jakobson, Roman. *O cheshskom stikhe, preimushchestvenno v sopostavlenii s russkim* [On Czech verse, primarily as compared to Russian]. Brown Slavic Reprint, no. 6. Providence: Brown University Press, 1969. See esp. pp. 102–12. Basic for Mayakovsky's versification.

————, and Sviatopolk-Mirsky, D. *Smert' Vladimira Mayakovskogo* [The death of Vladimir Mayakovsky]. The Hague: Mouton, 1975. Highly relevant to Mayakovsky's biography, especially his death.

Jangfeldt, Bengt, and Nilsson, Nils Åke, eds. *Vladimir Majakovskij: Memoirs and Essays*. Stockholm Studies in Russian Literature, no. 2. Stockholm: Almqvist & Wiksell, 1975. A collection of pieces by various authors on Mayakovsky's life and works.

————. *Majakovskij and Futurism, 1917–1921*. Stockholm: Almqvist & Viksell, 1976. A historical account of the events which led to Mayakovsky's transformation into a Soviet propaganda poet.

Kamensky, Vasily. *Zhizn's Mayakovskim* [Life with Mayakovsky]. Munich: Wilhelm Fink, 1974. Memoirs by one of the leading futurists and an early friend of Mayakovsky's.

Katanyan, Viktor. *Mayakovskii: Literaturnaya khronika* [Mayakovsky: a literary chronicle]. 4th rev. ed. Moscow: Goslitizdat, 1961. A day-by-day account of the biographical facts of Mayakovsky's life.

**Kemrad, Semyon.** *Mayakovskii v Amerike: Stranitsy biografii* [Mayakovsky in America: pages from his biography]. Moscow: Sovetskii pisatel', 1970. An account of Mayakovsky's visit to America in 1925.

**Khardzhiev, Nikolay, and Trenin, Vladimir.** *Poeticheskaya kul'tura Mayakovskogo* [Mayakovsky's poetic culture]. Moscow: Iskusstvo, 1970. Essays on various aspects of Mayakovsky's poetics, style, and literary connections.

**Livshits, Benedikt.** *The One and a Half-Eyed Archer.* Translated by John E. Bowlt. Newtonville, Mass.: Oriental Research Partners, 1977. These memoirs are highly relevant to Mayakovsky's early years as a futurist.

**Markov, Vladimir.** *Russian Futurism: A History.* Berkeley: University of California Press, 1968. The best account of Russian futurism in any language.

**Pertsov, Viktor.** *Mayakovskii: Zhizn' i tvorchestvo* [Mayakovsky: life and works]. 3d ed. 3 vols. Moscow: Nauka, 1976. The best "life and works" type study in Russian.

**Pitskel', Faina.** *Mayakovskii: Khudozhestvennoe postizhenie mira* [Mayakovsky: his creative understanding of the world]. Moscow: Nauka, 1979. An analytic treatment of Mayakovsky's poetics from a traditional viewpoint.

**Proffer, Ellendea, and Proffer, Carl R.** *The Ardis Anthology of Russian Futurism.* Ann Arbor: Ardis, 1980. Valuable for historical and literary background on Mayakovsky.

**Shklovsky, Viktor.** *Mayakovsky and His Circle.* Edited and translated by Lily Feiler. New York: Dodd, Mead, 1972. Valuable not only as a source for Mayakovsky's biography, but also for his development as a poet.

**Shtokmar, Mikhail.** *Rifma Mayakovskogo.* [Mayakovsky's rhymes]. Moscow: Sovetskii pisatel', 1958. The basic work on rhyme in Mayakovsky.

**Smirnov-Nesvitskii, Yurii.** *Zrelishche neobychaynoe: Mayakovskii i teatr* [An extraordinary spectacle: Mayakovsky and the theater]. Leningrad: Iskusstvo, 1975. An introduction to Mayakovsky's theater.

**Smorodin, A. A.** *Poeziya V. V. Mayakovskogo i publitsistika 20-kh godov.* [Mayakovsky's poetry and journalism of the 1920s]. Leningrad: Nauka, 1972. Important observations on the connections between Mayakovsky's poetry and political journalism in the 1920s.

**Stephan, Halina.** *"Lef" and the Left Front of the Arts.* Munich: Sagner, 1981. A detailed treatment of *Lef* and its relationships with organs of the Soviet state.

**Trenin, Vladimir.** *V masterskoy stikha Mayakovskogo* [In the workshop of Mayakovsky's verse]. Moscow: Sovetskii pisatel', 1978. Highly interesting observations on Mayakovsky's poetics and craftsmanship.

**Vinokur, Grigory.** *Mayakovskii—novator yazyka* [Mayakovsky: innovator of language]. Moscow: Sovetskii pisatel', 1943. Basic for an analysis of Mayakovsky's language.

**Williams, Robert C.** *Artists in Revolution: Portraits of the Russian Avant-Garde, 1905–1925.* Bloomington: Indiana University Press, 1977. Useful for background on Mayakovsky's activities as a poet and artist.

**Woroszylski, Wiktor.** *The Life of Mayakovsky.* Translated from the Polish by Boleslav Taborski. New York: Orion Press, 1970. A detailed account of Mayakovsky's life, presented through documents, letters, memoirs, and quotations from literary works.

# Index

(The works of Mayakovsky are listed under his name)

**DATE DUE**

| | | | |
|---|---|---|---|
| | | | |
| | | | |
| | | | |
| | | | |
| | | | |
| | | | |
| | | | |
| | | | |
| | | | |
| | | | |
| | | | |
| | | | |
| | | | |
| | | | |
| | | | |
| | | | |
| | | | |
| | | | |

DEMCO 38-297